WELCOME TO
RHYMING MIND

T.A.McALISTER

www.rhymingmind.com

arhymingmind@gmail.com

First Edition

Produced in New Zealand

Copyright © 2025 by T.A.McAlister
All rights reserved. Unique Poetry logo all rights reserved.
Names, characters, places and incidents are products of the author's imagination. The stories in this book are fictional and any resemblance to events or actual persons (living or dead) is purely coincidental. The opinions expressed do not necessarily reflect those of the author or publisher.
Without limiting the rights under copyright reserved above, no part of this publication may be reproduced, distributed, stored in or introduced into a retrieval system or transmitted in any form or by any means (electronic, mechanical, photocopying, recording or otherwise), without the prior written permission of the author.
Please note that no part of this book may be used or reproduced in any manner for the purpose of training artificial intelligence technologies or systems.

ISBN: 978-0-473-69904-8

Publisher: Rhyming Mind Ltd

**This book is dedicated to my son Michael,
who inspired me to be all that I can.**

"A thought can give you energy, a thought can be depleting,

A million thoughts run through our minds,

which one of them has meaning,

Can we determine right from wrong,

these thoughts that hold such power,

Send you insane thinking over again, relentless hour by hour,

But we are not our thoughts,

an entity to overcome,

Look at them objectively or your thoughts will overrun"

T.A.McAlister 19th January 2022

PREFACE

I knew I wasn't going to like it, facing the worst summer of my life,

Hoping my one way out of it, was producing the stories in my mind,

Four long years in the making, constantly working on getting it right,

The prospect of skin burn aching, gave me the courage to complete it this time,

A unique journey that occurred in my life, is being told to you now in this story,

Greatness can happen sometimes in plain sight, other times we're blind to its glory,

When I first started out in the world, like a sponge I took it all in,

And here is where my story reveals, how the shaping and learning begins,

So profoundly it was all taking place, somewhere deep in my mind,

Auburn haired and chubby faced, around three is where this was defined,

From very young, I remembered letters, every stroke and curve of their shape,

If it had a tail or it sat up high, and from this my mind would create,

For each letter had a style about it, there was something I just understood,

I stored that away, somewhere in my brain, and unleashed upon paper what I could,

There were many things still yet to uncover, the inner workings of my mind,

Scribbling away in crayons of colour, discovering my talent for rhyme,

But I wasn't the only family member who had poetic thoughts like this,

It makes me wonder if talent in parents can somehow be passed to their kids,

My Mum is the most avid reader and the best wordsmith I ever knew,

I would help her do the crossword teaser and had better answers as I grew,

My Dad has rhyming flair like me and gave me some of his work,

Said he wrote them around age thirteen, one day they might be of worth,

They're of great worth to me, so they're in this book that you are reading now,

Then in October of 2003, he wrote a song that captured crowds,

The True Kiwi Way became a big hit, so much so that some Kiwi's used,

His very song to help them along, in their campaign on national news,

It's awesome my Dad has a way with words, so is this where I got mine from,

Is this how my rhyming mind occurred, is it possible he passed it along,

Then lessons through school, evidently I found, helped make sense of what I could see,

Seeing each letter and knowing its sound, was the makings of what was to be,

Not all children think, so profoundly and deep, kids learn what they hear in rote,

But I was capturing and envisioning each, word as the sound was being spoke,

Spelling out each one quick in my mind and moving on to the next one I heard,

It was something I didn't quite know at the time, I had a knack and passion for words,

I can recall the lyrics to thousands of songs without even having to try,

They all just simply roll off my tongue, for the life of me I've never known why,

I remember the spelling of famous names, all because of how I can see,

The word in my mind, how it sits on the line, this recall just comes naturally,

"It starts with an H, a short name too, and the surname I know is quite long,

Not a common surname, its letters are low, and one is round with a tail on,"

That's me describing the thoughts in my head, every time that we played this game,

Remembering actors in our favourite movies, was to recall each one of their names,

My son would say, "you're getting real close, you've nearly spelled out the whole line,"

I could see every letter, every one of their strokes, until it finally popped into my mind,

"Halo Reeving," I shouted, "I knew I would click, he starred in Books Can Be Better,"

In just a few minutes, for it happens real quick, simply because I can see every letter,

The house we were in was not very big, but it was here that I started to write,

My 'Three Little Pigs' is where my journey begins, a poem that soon shaped my life,

It's sad but profound, and as I read it aloud, I vowed I'd make no more mistakes,

But I was still young, just turned thirty-one, and alas many more I did make,

Being rather proud, I printed it out, with some blue tack it was put on the fridge,

I didn't know at the time, but this poem of mine, would be the most special thing I did,

Then these words from my son, when I turned forty-one, who read it and made a suggestion,

"This poem I see, you're so proud you achieved, makes me wonder why you always question,

If it's something you like, why don't you just write, all your stories in rhyming words,

It might be a success, don't make this a regret, for years that's all I have heard,

Many people can't do, what comes natural to you, so buy a pad and put pen to paper,

And I don't want to hear, that you're scared and have fear, you can deal with all that shit later,

You taught me to spell by sounding out syllables, I spelled every word in the dictionary,

Your mind is unique, you rhyme as you speak, it's unorthodox and quite extraordinary,

I mastered hang man, won every competition, other parents don't do what you do,

I was a champion through primary, I had no derision, and it was all because of you,

Remember you said, each time that I read, something aloud your three-step rule,

If I got stuck on a word, sound it out so I heard, that made me the best speller at school,

You can do this Mum, your poems aren't dumb, they're unique, just put in the time,

Maybe this day next year, when you're feeling less fear, you can show someone all of your rhymes,"

And so things began, with words from my young man, telling me what I wrote in that poem,

I went back to the fridge, and reread what I did, and navigated my way through the unknown,

Of all my regrets, this was not to be one, I was determined to write this book,

So I heed the advice of my young son, giving me confidence was all it took,

And that is the story of my journey to glory, relaying it one step at a time,

Now I invite you to read my unique poetry and see inside a rhyming mind…

Three Little Pigs

One day, in my early twenties, there was a knock at the door.
It was Jealousy, so I let him in. Take a seat, I said. And he never moved.

After a decade of destruction, we were still going along together in my 30's
when there was another knock at the door. Hi, I'm Regret.
Come on in, I said. You can help prop up Jealousy. He's getting tired.

For the next decade Regret taught me to play the game Catch Up.
So distracted by this game I didn't hear a knock at the door.
But something crept in and sat quietly. Patiently.

My old friend Jealousy has now passed on, and Regret has moved
to play with another, when through the cracks my last guest appeared.

I'm the replacement, he said. You can call me Fear.
I'm by far the most deadly as I never make a sound.
You've only just realised I've always been around.

But don't worry, he said, with me you're not alone.
I linger in the cracks of every person's home.

Jealousy and Regret can be too hot headed
But I, however, am the one most dreaded.

Age and Wisdom think they can defy,
Patience is the answer but who makes time to try.

Emotions are a choice, a game of strength and will.
The stronger ones win over as the quiet ones stay still.

T.A.McAlister 8th May 2014

1   MOOSHY MIX

Recalling my youngest moment of not liking what was served,

My Dad made me a special meal, from my high chair I observed,

Sprinkled with sugar he sat beside me, thinking I would like this dish,

He began to proceed, but I did not heed to his culinary wish,

The first spoonful did not go in and neither did the next,

Slowly dribbling from my mouth, not sure what Dad expects,

This thickened goo, of mashed up food, he attempted to make sweet,

Was not a welcomed taste for me so I just sat there in my seat,

Spoonful after spoonful, but I never once engaged,

All of it just dribbled out, but I did not get enraged,

My bib was catching most of it and the rest fell on my shirt,

I much preferred the garden variety of eating worms and dirt,

But he persevered as I kept my cool, each spoonful dribbling out,

His patience wearing very thin, as he started to pace about,

Mum warned him from the very start that I would not concede,

Quietly stubborn, I remained determined, but he insisted that I feed,

Upon this meal he thought I'd like because he liked it too,

He took his time to realise that I would not eat this food,

I stayed in my chair, as he pulled out his hair, and the battle of wills was complete,

He walked away in a huff that day, because he had to admit defeat,

The food went cold, but he could not scold my refusal for a mooshy mix,

A stubborn, determined two year old who just did not like wheat stix…

2   BREAKFAST DINNER

My relationship with food has never been that great,

Starting with those dreaded words, 'eat everything on your plate,'

Well firstly I only liked half of it, so the other half always went cold,

Poking and prodding at what remained, trying to do as I was told,

So I smothered it all with tomato sauce, in an attempt to make it blend,

Disguising cold boiled cabbage in a sea of thickened red,

There wasn't a dog under our dining table that I could feed scraps to,

I had to stay there in my chair until I'd eaten all my food,

Was this some kind of pay back, from that day in my high chair,

When I refused to eat that mooshy mix and Dad pulled out his hair,

Now here I am at the dining table and must eat what's on my dish,

Dad said he means business now and won't take any shit,

So dessert was served and polished off, while I sat finishing my tea,

My siblings had left the table because they were tired of waiting for me,

And if I didn't eat my dinner that night it was served to me in the morning,

Dried out day old tomato sauce got worse from microwave warming,

It was a battle of wills again, as I looked at my breakfast dinner,

Dry retching sounds as I spread it around, in my attempt to make it thinner,

I mastered this lesson many times before it never happened again,

For the beauty of being a middle child meant I got my way in the end…

3   DINING OUT

Dining in a restaurant was all about food to me,
But my sister was far more interested in the room of personal hygiene,
The moment our family was seated, she would ask to be excused,
She always felt compelled to inspect the state of the powder room,
Darting off with head held high, she'd prance past all the seats,
Never mind the delicious menu with its list of tasty treats,
Her needs were simply met, upon entering the loo,
This was of great importance and something she had to do,
As we gazed at all the options, waiting for her return,
I knew what I was having, even eyed up their desserts,
My sister's fetish with toilets, continued throughout the meal,
I saw these opportunities for a few chips that I could steal,
After several dinner outings, this notion soon caught on,
Maybe there's something in this, so next time I went along,
First there was just two of us and then it was all three,
Mum and Dad left sitting there while their girls went off to pee,
Prancing through the restaurant, with intent of washing our hands,
The final destination was like being in a fantasy land,
We would giggle away, as we casually played, with all the many cool things,
I never realised that toilet time was entertainment for young offspring,
The little soaps and folded towels, we used up all we could,
I never dreamed, or even thought, powder rooms could be this good,
Our patient parents never questioned, they just ordered some more wine,
While us three girls just fluffed about, taking our sweet time,
When we left this happy place and resumed again our seats,
Content to finish our dinner meal and move on to ordering sweets,
Our dining out experience became less about the food,
And more about the enjoyment of checking out the restaurant loos...

4   HOLIDAY CAKE

My favourite days growing up were always school holidays,
Three young girls in the kitchen, making food was great child's play,
We'd get out all the ingredients to make a chocolate cake,
But the mixture was always half eaten, before it had a chance to bake,
We would sneak back in, open the oven, and eat it out of the tin,
The half cooked runny cake mixture was getting very thin,
Suffice to say, the cake was small and struggled to really cook,
We kept spooning out more and more, telling Mum we were having a look,
She never put up a protest or scolded us for eating,
A cake that didn't rise at all was still good enough for keeping,
We loved the mixture so damn much we decided one day to try,
Consuming the entire contents of a chocolate mix we'd buy,
So we beat two eggs and the mix together, without the oven being on,
The three of us sat around the bowl, scraping and licking till it was gone,
It sounded like a great idea until our bellies started to hurt,
Reminded me of when I was three out in the garden eating dirt,
We struggled to get to sleep that night due to our bloated tummies,
We just had to eat all the uncooked cake because it tasted so yummy,
I'm pleased to say it was on this day that we never did it again,
We learned our lesson that cakes are best cooked right through to the end,
It's funny how children have some idea that seems good at the time,
And funnier still is the fact that premix remained a favourite of mine…

5   EAT WITH YOUR EYES

As I slowly grew, my relationship with food didn't really show on my waist,

I chose certain meals, that simply appealed to my eyes and not my tastes,

I'd ask my Mum everywhere we went, "do you think that I'll like this?"

Oysters Kilpatrick looked good in the picture, but not really a children's dish,

We were at the beach, getting something to eat at the busiest place in town,

All day in the sun, burning white skin was fun, in the attempt of one day being brown,

I remember this place it was on the corner, a restaurant by the seaside,

Covered in sand, and still not tanned, they sold seafood of every kind,

I knew I liked bacon and the picture looked good, upon their shiny menu,

I was so impressed with my young self, ordering oysters at a fancy venue,

Then smelly hard shells appeared before me, with only a few strips of bacon,

I knew in that moment I wouldn't like them and felt my tummy achin',

I should have ordered the fish and chips now I'm stuck with a meal I dislike,

Dad saw my displeasure, so he fixed my error, and ordered me something I liked,

So the wobbly critters on my plate became an entrée for our Mum,

She wouldn't let them go to waste, she thought these things were yum,

This lesson I learned, as my stomach still churned, I dared never order again,

Don't eat with your eyes, for it may be disguised by a picture that's all pretend…

6   CURRENCY OF SWEETS

Being allowed to buy our lunch at school was a privilege growing up,

If you happened to find a coin or two, then that was sheer damn luck,

It was the same for chocolate in our house, harder than finding hen's teeth,

It was always kept on the highest shelf, far away from children's reach,

And especially from me, as I was to be, always looking for something sweet,

Hunting around for coins unfound, that could buy me a nice school treat,

So to find some lost and lonely coins in pockets, bags or cars,

Was seen as a trade, for the sweetness I craved, in the form of a chocolate bar,

Taking my coins to school the next day, I'd be the first in line,

At the little shop, where I delightfully swapped, all the coins that I could find,

One and two cent lolly bags, you could buy quite a lot back then,

Have plenty enough for yourself and some left over for your friends,

Until one day I hit the jackpot, it was music to my ears,

Mum signed up to our school tuck shop as a parent volunteer,

I was over the moon at this wonderful plan,

Dreamed of the sweets in the palm of my hand,

Gone were the days of searching for money,

My lunch times were made because of my Mummy,

It no longer mattered if I was first or last,
I walked straight to the counter and the line-ups I passed,
Waiting in there was a brown bag for me,
It contained a big sandwich and all kinds of sweets,
Caramels, carobs and lollies hard boiled,
Those lunch times at school I was completely spoiled,
But I shared my good fortune with my best friends,
And my relationship with food began to transcend,
I learned in my youth if I stored treats away,
I could sweeten my tooth on those rainy days,
When there was none in the house and I needed to barter,
Wise to the motto, work smarter not harder,
Stashed in my room or some out on loan,
I learned the currency of sweets from living at home…

7   MY ARCH NEMESIS

My love for chocolate became so widely known that more people hid it from me,

I would eat the whole block, as I just couldn't stop, at eating one little piece,

My desire and need, turned from pleasure to greed, especially at Easter time,

The bunny laid eggs at the end of my bed, as I woke in the morning to find,

I was the first to get up and had to be quiet so no one heard my racket,

As I basked in the joy of devouring all the chocolate there was in the packet,

When my sisters arose they saw on their bed what the bunny had left behind,

But I wasn't allowed to ask them to share just because I ate all of mine,

It always took Tarn so many days to eat her big chocolate bundle,

I'd sneak a big piece and hide it away, but just get myself into trouble,

She was little you see, so it was easy for me, but Mum was always on guard,

So I'd make up a lie, for despite how I tried, going undetected was really hard,

But I wasn't concerned about being punished or told off in any way,

Any reprimand I simply rubbished, they could say all they wanted to say,

But my parents were smart and far more cunning, as they discovered my only weakness,

It was out of control my love and fondness for that decadent taste of sweetness,

What they discovered, that had me buggered, was a chocolate filled with crème,

I could not scoop, out all the goop, from each piece filled orange or green,

My arch nemesis, their favourite snack, was revolting, sickly stuff,

My futile efforts to remove the filling didn't work, so I simply gave up,

So this chocolate block was placed in the pantry, right there on the middle shelf,

Reassured it was safe, because I disliked the taste, hence I kept my hands to myself,

I recall this moment rather fondly, as if it were yesterday,

My parents found a chocolate block, that finally kept my cravings at bay…

8   THE ART OF TRADING FOOD

The relationship I had with food somewhat got a little better,

But when you live with two hundred girls, it really didn't matter,

You had to eat whatever was served or simply go without,

'Take it or leave it' was the motto, in all boarding schools, no doubt,

They were strict at every meal time, for you had to make a presence,

Formally dressed in school attire and line up like hungry peasants,

If you were last, by any chance, the trays of food got thinner,

This is where I perfected, all my bartering skills at dinner,

I'd pile on my plate, food I never ate, and used this as a tool,

To trade that night for food I liked, was the secret unwritten rule,

It was never discussed with the girls as such, it was just something that we did,

Stashed in the corner of all our rooms were the goodies that we hid,

We were only allowed out on a Sunday, for exactly two whole hours,

Run to the shop, fill our bags to the top, walk back and have it all devoured,

So when it came to stashing treats, they were few and far between,

Pretend you had finished your bag and keep the remainder completely unseen,

But it wasn't the ants or even the flies, that we hid our stash from prying eyes,

'Twas the matrons we'd snub, if they found our sweet grub, and took our stashed supplies,

When I recall these days and remember when, the time I was at boarding school,

I laugh to myself and think of my friends and that priceless unwritten rule,

The bartering we all secretly did, with food back in those days,

If you were last, and forced to fast, you'd better have something to trade,

Of all the lessons I learned in school, this lesson proved most worth it,

The art of trading food for sweets, I now have down pat and perfect…

9 FIRST KISS

The question that burned on school kids' lips, was the desire to know if you've ever been kissed,

I always thought that part sounded easy, it was third base that I was scared,

How does one know, where all the parts go and what to do when you're finally there,

You could see my young mind ticking over and the innocence in my eyes,

Unsure of what sex was all about, far too young for that in my life,

But the topic was always trending, as I went through primary school,

Sometimes it was best, to just say yes and make out you knew all the rules,

If you had an older sibling, there was a chance you could learn from them,

Otherwise, it was up to you to find out from your parents or friends,

So to answer the burning question, do you remember your first kiss,

I remember mine so vividly, I was so nervous that I nearly missed,

But I was a really late bloomer and didn't see the need for it yet,

The only kissing I had known was my family's sloppy cheek pecks,

It wasn't till I was in high school that I learned what a kiss was to be,

A close embrace, touching face to face and this moment I had at thirteen,

I was thankful to my school friends, who had experienced it several times,

They advised I practice on a pillow so I had it rehearsed in my mind,

I was so proud of my effort in trying, after the weird advice I was given,

I parted my lips like they told me, closed my eyes and moved into position,

But I couldn't see a bloody thing and my legs then started to shake,

My heart was beating out of my chest, when I felt these lips on my face,

Tender, soft and gentle, he knew precisely what to do,

I was so nervous I damn near froze, I stayed still and didn't move,

Kissing someone for the very first time is a moment I'll never forget,

It didn't last as long as I thought, but at least it wasn't sloppy and wet,

I went to school the following Monday and proudly told all my mates,

That cute blonde boy from the skating rink kissed me at the side entrance gate,

Of course they paid little attention, all my friends were so far advanced,

But at least I'd moved on from pillows and was finally given the chance,

To experience what it was like and actually know how to kiss,

I've done it many times since then and pleased to say, I no longer miss…

10   SCHOOL BOYS' DREAM

As a teenager I had many wonderful times and I experienced these days in the city,

Dressed to the nines, in a restaurant to dine, with my friend looking both very pretty,

After dinner we walked, into town as we talked, about maybe hitching a ride,

So we stuck out our thumbs, just for some fun, then this car pulled up at our side,

A couple of boys, in a red two door toy, spotted us walking alone,

The car smelled of booze, and we had nothing to lose, so hopped in and drove down the road,

It was the perfect scene, a school boys' dream, two girls getting into their car,

We may have been young, but we were far from dumb, and town wasn't really that far,

We drank their wine, and had a good time, driving through town on this memorable night,

That's when we stopped, in a secluded spot, well out of everyone's sight,

I was up front, my friend in the back, with a boy that she hardly knew,

They got out of their seats, walked a few feet, so he could make his next move,

I didn't go far, I just stayed in the car, with the driver who rolled up a smoke,

He chopped up a brew, that I'd seen once or two, a mixture of tobacco and dope,

It wasn't that long, my friend was gone, thought she'd return a got-lucky chick,

But this was not the case, from the state of her face, it was sore from the guy she was with,

The whiskers he had, turned out to be bad, and the kissing made her lips very red,

We were dropped home that night, but by morning's first light, she refused to get out of bed,

Her cracked peeling lips, were impossible to miss, so we had to come up with a lie,

No one was to know, about the guy with the mow, so she said she ate a hot pie,

The worst part for me, was that I had to be, the culprit that pushed it in place,

Said we were mucking around, last night whilst in town, and I shoved this hot pie in her face,

Our friends were not pleased, at the thought I could be, so cruel to my mate of four years,

But I did this for her, took the blame and the hurt, to avoid the ridicule she feared,

But we did have some laughs, about her painful moustache, but the truth we always kept hidden,

It was just between us, and me she could trust, so of course, all was forgiven,

As the years went on, we slowly lost touch, but I often think about Deb,

And that night we hitchhiked, with two boys by moonlight, and the bullshit story we said…

CHOCOLATE AFFAIR

This explosion in my mouth
is really quite sublime,
Every part of me comes to life
it simply blows my mind,
Words cannot express
the way you make me feel,
The power you have over me
is truly quite surreal,
I weaken in your presence
so smooth and silky brown,
Stunned as I'm caressed
I can feel you going down,
My senses going crazy
heart quickens with each beat,
Your taste is on my tongue
as blood rushes to my cheeks,
You slide inside so easily
and taunt me with that look,
I just can't get enough of you
first time was all it took,
Come and fill me up again
you're such delicious stuff,
My decadent, splendid, sweetest friend
I can never get enough…

THE SWEETEST SOUND

Come in a little bit closer
there's a sound you don't want to miss,
A moment so sweet and tender
is the sound of our first kiss,
You press yourself into me
I let out a gentle sigh,
My heart is beating faster
emotions running high,
This sound is like no other
two people long to share,
I press myself into you
run my fingers through your hair,
You whisper gently to me
softly as you speak,
I feel my entire body
slowly turning weak,
I close my eyes as you pull me near
and feel your warm embrace,
I taste your lips and hear the sound
of kisses on my face,
Come in a little bit closer
there's a sound you don't want to miss,
The sound that turns me on
is the sound of our first kiss…

13   DARRYLL FROM THE BARREL

For most young children growing up it was their parents that worked in clubs,

But for me and my sisters, our parents insisted, we work in their newly bought pub,

It was right on the corner, at the end of Main Street, in a popular lakeside town,

It offered a selection of good hearty meals and boasted the best beer around,

Word soon got out, the pub had new owners, so folks came in droves to inspect,

Dad was known as 'Darryll from The Barrel', but not the type of publican you'd expect,

Kind hearted and generous, hospitable in nature and told many a tale that was funny,

He was the best damn thing, that pub had ever seen, and boy, he knew how to make money,

The party would start as soon as we opened and finish the next day around dawn,

The drinks were cheap, people spilled onto the street, and between many punters he was torn,

Everyone wanted to drink with Darryll, get on the piss with this guy from The Barrel, meet his wife and three beautiful girls,

From that moment on, our family belonged, and that pub changed our entire world,

As the three of us grew, Toni and I poured the brew, whilst Tarn helped Mum in the kitchen,

Too little by far, to work in the bar, but damn, she cooked spectacular dishes,

By the age of thirteen, she was hard, fast and mean, at pumping meals out by the hour,

And to the patrons' surprise, these little blue eyes, would appear from behind the counter,

We had the place sussed, between the five of us, and the people just kept pouring in,

From towns near and far, to come to our bar, where they heard the best parties begin,

My relationship with food, got swapped out for the booze and by this stage I was almost twenty,

Many boys were about, traded their money to shout, me as many drinks as I could empty,

There were no problems there, as they stepped into my lair, to realise they were never alone,

All I had to do, was keep pouring brew, till they fell over and I simply went home,

I look back on this now and I feel rather proud, of the many invitations that I got,

But being a young girl, in the bar business world, those drunken moments were easily forgot,

I've thought many times, about this past of mine and reminisce over stories we told,

Punters had the best life, dancing drunk many nights, with a family born to rock and roll…

The Red Barrel, Taupo 1993

14 BIG CITY

I may have worked in a pub, but to access nightclubs, you could not get in at nineteen,

You had to be twenty one, to have any fun, and experience the drinking scene,

So I ventured out into town one night, with my friend who was the same age as me,

Having worked for a while, I knew our looks and our smile, would get us in to the club of her dreams,

It was a popular place, packed to the brim, I worked my magic and they let us both in, after that we let our hair down,

Young, pretty, and underage, a DJ playing on the stage, then we lost each other in the crowd,

It would have been at least an hour or so before we found one another again,

She was up on stage, just dancing away, that's how I spotted my half naked friend,

She was blonde, tall and having a ball, as I watched from down on the floor,

She was on a mission, with this guy she was kissin', who probably thought he would score,

Rachel and I were really good mates, so she gestured I join her on stage,

She was leading him on, often showing her thong, to a man at least twice her age,

Next thing I know, she was moving in close and pretended to then kiss me,

She knew I'd respond, so I just played along and together we danced and teased,

The guys on the floor, were shouting for more, from the way we were both dancing dirty,

She undid her blouse, and waived it around, having fun just teasing and flirting,

It was all just for show, but these guys didn't know, we were friends all through high school,

We snuck into a place, with the smile on our face, so that night we broke all the rules,

We went back to her house and continued to party, for Rachel was now on a roll,

She had a small flat in the middle of town and a deal she had to uphold,

If I get us in to the club of your dreams, then you must do something for me,

When you pack your bags to leave this place and finally head overseas,

I want you to go to a busy nightclub and do what we did up on stage,

I'd like to know, if you can steal the show, with your looks and being underage,

At the end of the year Rachel went overseas and I asked her how she got on,

When you're real tall and pretty in a big foreign city, she had no problems at all being blonde…

15   RACE TO THIRD BASE

Not everyone I ask remembers their first kiss, but they all remember reaching third base,

As I was growing up, many teens were in a rush, like it was some kind of medal winning race,

Well I was not in a hurry, to share my milk and honey, with just any old random guy,

It had to be real with the feelings I feel, but I was certainly willing to try,

I heard many stories, about this moment of glory, though the boys only wanted one thing,

So keep yourself clothed, till the day he propose, and you're wearing his wedding ring,

How long will that bloody take, I'm not sure I can wait, I've outgrown this virginity,

I knew one girl at twelve, who had already delved, and here I was at friggin' eighteen,

The man that I chose, thankfully did not propose, but he was my choice for the play,

With nice compliments and pretty gifts, it was with him that I went all the way,

If I could ever have that moment again, I would have chosen a far better spot,

Ordered some wine, and just took our time, and not kept looking at the damn clock,

Gyratin' and twistin', getting into position, that he said was great for your partner,

Being my first time, I had no clue in mind, and this guy just kept getting faster,

So I held on tight, for the ride of my life, our bodies entwined together,

He wasn't real long, but man he was strong, it was like he could just go forever,

I looked back at the clock, be nice if we stopped, took a break and wiped off the sweat,

But he just picked me up, there's no time to disrupt, as the gyratin' was not over yet,

It was the middle of summer, and I needed some slumber, in that moment we finally did part,

I laid there so sweetly, in his arms nestled neatly, so was shocked when he let out a fart,

In the most unromantic of ways, we finished our play, from the eruption that came from his arse,

No blankets or sheets, to wave away the foul reek, never before had I moved so damn fast,

So I thanked mister cutie, for the midsummer booty, and I too left him with a gift,

He was not prepared, as he lay unaware, of the deadly silent one I let rip,

As he was gasping for air, I made for the stairs, because that was my worst one yet,

Smiling all the way home, proud to have shown a secret weapon he would never forget…

16   THIRTY YEARS AGO

Thirty years ago, back in the nineties, I was in the last stage of my teens,

I was so new to sex, living sheltered I guess, you could say I was naïve and green,

Then I worked in a bar, with me old ma and pa, and learned the ways of the world,

I saw way back then, how quickly most men, were attracted to good looking girls,

So in turn I learned, despite what I yearned, I wasn't what they wanted to see,

I was scarred from the sun, yet still lots of fun, just not endowed with any beauty,

School lessons on sex, were never the best, but I learned as time had moved on,

That sometimes in life we may get it right, but mostly I just got it wrong,

So I became rather wary, of any man caring, because I understood crystal clear,

It was not my looks, for the reason they shook, my Dad's hand in an attempt to get near,

Was it just my folks bar, they offered rings and a car, were they simply just after the money,

Didn't believe what they said, kept to myself instead, for I knew I was no gorgeous honey,

As this wariness grew, my partners were few, and I buried my feelings underground,

Being unable to trust, the walls just built up, until one day a young man broke them down,

He opened up doors, and I was wary no more, for he showed me to first love myself,

I'd spent so many years, frozen with fear, evidently putting my life on the shelf,

Was I simply too quick, to dismiss that first kiss, from any man that I ever met,

It was so long ago, so I really don't know, but it's something I sometimes regret,

That young man today, still calls me to say, you're always my special someone,

It was true love from him, my wounds healed within, I found love through raising my son,

If only I'd known, all those years ago, that it was never something to fear,

When I gave him my heart, he quietly sparked, something in me truly sincere,

All that time I'd been thinking, drowning and sinking, longing to be who I am,

It took being a mum, for me to know love was always in the palm of my hand…

17   JOE THE DOG

As three young girls growing up we had many pets to adore,

But one that stole our three hearts was the tiniest one of all,

A small long haired Chihuahua, Joe the Dog became his name,

A pet unlike any other, so we included him in all our games,

Being so small he fit on one hand the day Dad brought him home,

And always from that moment on, he would never be alone,

We carried him around, everywhere in our arms, any moment that we could,

Very rarely did he see the ground, but of course, sometimes he would,

My sisters and I would fuss each night over who was sleeping with Joe,

Snuggle him down under our covers hoping that he wouldn't go,

For if he got out, we all knew he was sleeping somewhere else instead,

We were not allowed to leave our rooms and bring him back to our beds,

We adored him so much we doted on him like he was one of our dolls,

Bathed him in the tub with us until the warm bath went cold,

Then dress him up, in our dolls stuff, in frilly clothes of pink,

We even managed to curl his fur, as it was long enough to crimp,

His ears were soft with hair so long, so we'd also plait those too,

Hang pegs off his plaits, got in trouble for that, there was nothing we didn't do,

Joe was loved and completely adored by all us three young girls,

He was our most favourite pet of all, in the whole entire world,

When Tarn got a pram for Christmas, to push around her many toys,

We saw this opportunity as something our pets could also enjoy,

So we got our other two animals, Beautiful Blackie and Ginger cat,

Placed them in the pram with Joe, if only they both stayed and sat,

Blackie would scratch and make her escape, whereas Ginger happily laid,

Right there asleep next to Joe, as we pushed the pram and played,

It was big enough for the two of them as well as a few teddy bears,

Why get out and use their legs when three girls pushed them everywhere,

Joe the Dog, who rarely saw the ground, and was carried by us every day,

Would go into our rooms and mope around, when we went to Nana's to stay,

Our beautiful brown Chihuahua, that we smothered with love and care,

Missed us so unbearably, he knew the moment we weren't there,

When we returned, he'd come running so fast, and be yappin' up a storm,

He knew he had stolen our three hearts and it was in our arms he belonged…

18   GINGER THE BRAVE TOMCAT

The ginger cat that was in our lives, was a few years old before us kids arrived,

Strong, agile, fearsome and scary, left many an animal cautious and wary,

Like this one cold evening on a moonlit night, my parents woke to a howling fright,

Three big dogs were by the door, and felt the wrath of Gingers' claws,

He bowled them up in a corner so tight they could not get away,

Too terrified to try and make an escape were two Alsatians and one Great Dane,

They were lost, cold and hungry, when they spotted a bowl of food,

But Ginger had other plans for this wandering canine brood,

He may have been a docile tom to our family of three young kids,

But if any strays made their way, from the shadows he no longer hid,

He made it known to all that roamed, don't mess with a ginger tom,

I may get pushed around in a pram, but my claws are fast and strong,

He would go into battle to protect himself as well as his small territory,

But there was this night when a hungry fox made an attempt to steal his glory,

It scaled the fence into our yard and quickly Ginger was snatched,

Dad heard the most dreadful of sounds coming from our brave tomcat,

Dad's presence scared the fox away, but Ginger was still in his mouth,

Unable to jump the fence and escape, he released him and headed south,

Poor old Ginge was badly bruised, so laid down in a cardboard box,

In front of the fire he never moved, his back was badly squashed,

A narrow escape, you'd think he'd learn, but protection was in his nature,

Before too long, our fearsome tom was again in the face of danger,

He chased a possum up a tree, clawed and hissed a great defence,

But this time there was no protection, from Dad or a backyard fence,

He was on his own and came back home, drenched in blood and much saliva,

His paws were squashed, his fur was mangled, but Ginge was a true survivor,

Sore and bruised, he limped into the room and laid himself down on the floor,

He was back in the box in front of the fire, licking his wounds and bloodied paws,

And so it appeared, he had little fear and continued to test his nine lives,

So he ventured around, found this hole in the ground, and had a look for what was inside,

Well my oh my, to his surprise, he struck gold with a litter of kittens,

But the big brave tom had it all wrong, for the doe was not at all smitten,

She latched onto Ginge and the clash begins, her sharp teeth outweighing his claws,

He yowled out to escape, but the rabbit laid waste, half his body was now in her jaws,

This big mummy doe would not let him go, so Ginger just ran for his life,

He was finally released, as she made her retreat, but boy did he put up a fight,

As time went on, us kids had grown hearing stories of his remarkable past,

The lion in him, the ferocious Ginge, was exceptional and lightning fast,

Any wandering brood, that came into view, quickly learned the rules of the game,

This small orange creature, was a feisty hard teacher and Ginge knew how to cause pain,

But we knew him as a big fat cat whom we loved and doted upon,

He slowly aged, so his battling days were all over and long gone,

He teased and taunt, clawed and fought, he was the undefeated champ,

Suffice to say, he was happy to lay with his pampered life in a pram…

19   RUN FOR YOUR LIFE

From the days of being a child and growing up with so many pets,

I've since had a few of my own, but didn't turn out the way I expect,

We had a kitten that kept running away and gold fish that died in a bowl,

I bought these pets for my little boy when he was just four years old,

Then we adopted a small black dog that we decided to call Peso,

Tenacious and cunningly natured, she was forced to stay on the go,

She had to learn quickly that her only friend was also her only rival,

She was never going to be very big, so speed was her way of survival,

I taught my son to bounce the ball and play fetch as a friendly game,

Be gentle, Peso is only small, and be mindful where you aim,

Well Michael was just as tenacious and would throw his toys instead,

A large octopus made of plastic and hold it high up over his head,

The toys were always much bigger than Peso could ever pick up,

So the game of fetch was impossible and Michael could be quite rough,

He knew his throw was limited, so he would bang the toys on the floor,

There was nothing for Peso to catch, but she always came back for more,

I didn't condone his behaviour and looked out for Peso each day,

Michael throwing his toys too hard and forcing Peso out of the way,

But they played like this for hours, running through every room in the house,

Peso never took off or cowered, she was as fast as a little church mouse,

She found many places to hide, so she had the game down pat,

When she saw Michael's arm raised high, and the octopus aiming to splat,

She knew she only really needed, enough time to make an escape,

The distance of about three metres, where she stood to anxiously wait,

As the octopus came flying, she would dart off under a bed,

I commend her efforts in trying, to catch something that was aimed for her head,

But the little wee dog never gave up, unless she came to me for a rest,

Her guaranteed place of sanctuary was next to me, right by my legs,

She'd grab a drink and catch her breath, then play again with the toy of death, dodging tentacles that were always inbound,

Michael would laugh, as Peso ran past, waving the octopus and chasing her around,

They played like this throughout the day, but when evening started to fall,

I'd tuck Mikes into bed, put Peso away, and give her a break from it all,

But as Mikes grew, the rules he knew, that if Peso stood by my legs,

He was not allowed to pull her out nor aim anything at her head,

They actually got on, like two peas in a pod, even though their play was quite strange,

The idea of dodgeball octopus became both their favourite game,

Peso missed him when he went to school, a little lonely she would feel,

But as soon as Michael bowled through the door, the octopus was hot on her heels,

I often think about old Peso, and recall these moments with Mikes,

The tenacity of such a small creature, who mastered the game of 'run for your life'...

20   THIS LITTLE PIGGY

This little piggy went to market, then little piggy followed him home,

He saw the knives being sharpened, to skin him right down to the bone,

This little piggy happened to see, as he looked at his little pink feet,

And cried out wee wee wee, at the thought of becoming cooked meat,

So smart little piggy went oink oink, then opened his mouth to talk,

"Fetch the piggy who had roast beef, go turn that fat piggy into pork,"

The farmer turned to little piggy, stunned he was able to speak,

"I'll glaze your skin till it's crispy, in the oven along with the beef,

Bake potatoes and carrots as well, and put an apple inside your mouth,

Salivate at the delicious smell, of you roasting all through my house,"

Little piggy then had an idea, to avoid being the farmers' dinner,

Through a gap he then disappeared, for he was somewhat thinner,

He ran through the house as fast as he could, escaped in the nick of time,

Little piggy ran straight into the woods, but the farmer was right behind,

Puffing and panting, but he did not stop, until he came to a house made of bricks,

The farmer was carrying an axe he would chop, little piggy into tiny wee bits,

This house in the woods, that piggy ran to, had a big bad wolf inside,

He was making a pot of tasty pork stew, so piggy ran away for his life,

The farmer searched all through the night, wielding an axe and large pitchfork,

But little piggy just stayed out of sight, and away from the light of his torch,

When piggy woke up in the early morn, he wondered what next he should do,

If he stayed in the woods anywhere after dawn, he'd be found and turned into stew,

So little piggy went back to market, and sought refuge behind a large stall,

The owner had long since departed, now the daughter took care of it all,

She was perched up high on her tuffet, eating her curds and whey,

When the eyes of little Miss Muffet, spotted piggy in amongst all the hay,

She said to herself, "this little piggy could help," and gestured he come sit beside her,

"A creature like you, is too good to be stewed, you can scare away all of the spiders,"

So now little piggy had a new home, far away from the farmers' pitchfork,

Lots of room and gardens to roam, no danger of being cooked for roast pork,

Now when little piggy goes to market, he's the most doted on pig in the square,

Miss Muffet trotted off to fill her basket, when she saw this old man stop to stare,

When the farmer saw piggy all happy and fat, he raised his arm to the sky,

Drew it back down and swung his great axe, yelling, "that little piggy is mine,"

A crowd gathered quickly to watch the display, but Miss Muffet had other ideas,

She grabbed hold of the farmer and pushed him away, for it was only spiders she feared,

"Get away from my swine, that little piggy is mine, I took him in for my very own,"

The farmer swallowed his pride, and ran off as he cried, wee wee wee all the way home…

21   FRESH IS BEST

There's an art to picking up horse poop, and you may think this absurd,
But after two months of many a scoop, there's a few things that I learned,
Firstly, you must place the pick, in precisely the right spot,
To avoid any double handling or accidentally dropping the lot,
And always be mindful of grass, as you put the pick into place,
For if anyone saw they would laugh, as they watched poop fling into your face,
You may think you've got the whole load, but hooked around one of the spikes,
Is a loop in the grass, you didn't get past, and explodes if the poop isn't ripe,
So the easiest ones of all, are the poops that are just laid fresh,
Perfectly piled and positioned, to be the best damn scoop you can get,
It's the pony's that have the smallest, of all the poop, as I understand,
But these don't always go on, so I pick the rest up with my hand,
For these littlest ones are sometimes tricky, and often fall through the gap,
But the biggest ones, heavy and sticky, wreak havoc on your lower back,
It's also best I noticed, to pick as much as you can first round,
For if you go back for seconds, the first lot just falls to the ground,
Forget about ever re-scooping, because that just falls to the side,
Believe me I know what I'm doing, and want it done in the quickest time,
With all that I learned on the field, I've shared with you what I observed,
If you want the most from your yield, remember the art of picking up turds…

LITTLE LOUIE

You walked away from me last night and not a word was spoken,

Into the arms of another woman, my days empty and broken,

You tugged at all my heart strings and I played to every tune,

If only I had known, those were my last moments with you,

I would have held you in my arms and never let you go,

Kissed you more and showed you all the love I had to show,

But I know this woman very well and know she'll treat you right,

My beautiful Louie that I adore and cuddled every night,

I rescued you from the puppy lions and brought you to my home,

So much love I have for you, I wanted you for my own,

Your adorable face and floppy ears and gorgeous jet black eyes,

Won me over the day we met, even I was quite surprised,

How such a tiny creature, could ever win my heart,

I was warned not to fall for you, but I loved you from the start,

I poked my finger through your cage and called you Little One,

You heard my voice and out you came as fast as you could run,

I couldn't control my feelings or contain them in any way,

When I fell in love with you, I just wanted you to stay,

So I wish my Little Louie, all the best in his new home,

Knowing that you're right next door means I get to see you grow,

You may think that I've left you or that I've gone away,

But I could never leave you Louie,

I'm right here for you every day…

23   IF LOUIE WAS MINE

I'd like to propose for just one last time, that I take on Louie and he always be mine,

I will fix him and vax him, do whatever it takes, call him my own and a life I will make,

Together with him for the rest of his days, take care of his needs till he rests in his grave,

I will love him and squeeze him and smother with kisses, take him for walks or whatever he wishes,

He will be by my side through all thick and thin, fill the void in my life that I feel deep within,

I will teach him to fetch and return me the ball, devote all my time to this creature so small,

He will not bark incessantly at cats or windows, he will be well behaved wherever I go,

All it takes is some love, some training and time, I will do all these things if Louie was mine,

So I offer again my proposal idea, my heart yearns each day for him to be here,

I just can't let go of my Little One Louie, I'd be over the moon if you just left him to me,

I will pay for his shots and then pay you some more, I just can't keep watching him walk out my door,

I adored him so much from the first day we met, this tiny small creature I want as my pet,

So please do consider, keep my proposal in mind, I need to know soon before we run out of time,

Every day he gets bigger and needs just one home, I propose that be mine and I make him my own…

24 MOVING ORNAMENT

I cried and cried for you last night, regretting the decision I made,

Thinking I had to give you up as I reluctantly gave you away,

Apparently I couldn't meet your needs, but it turns out I actually could,

I should've fought harder for you and me, I could have and still should,

They say that time heals all our wounds, but my wounds will never heal,

I found you first and loved you most, it'll always be the way I feel,

It's never too late to take you back and arrange that we be together,

Undo the hurt and pain I can't hack and have you with me forever,

I would never tie you to a post or stuff you in a cage,

You'd be at my side as I lovingly stroked your silky coat each day,

But I watch you live behind a gate and run along the fence,

You're just a moving ornament and to me that makes no sense,

You're not just a dog, you're a beautiful creature, the most wonderful thing in the world,

Your adorable eyes and little fine features, you made me the happiest girl,

So my heart just breaks more and more, and I struggle to get through the day,

To know you're alone in the house next door is the most unbearable pain,

So I bide my time and wait for you, in hope that one day you'll be,

By my side, with a love that's true, where you belong is here with me…

25   LITTLE ONE BIG ONE NOW

My beautiful Little Louie, oh how much you have grown,
The hardest decision I ever made, was having to let you go,
I see you walk past every day, and I long to have you near,
I hear your bark from a mile away, wishing you were here,
But I couldn't offer the things she can, or the life you need,
To keep you captive in my room, was only all about me,
So I put my feelings aside and thought what was best for you,
The house next door with two small dogs, was the best thing I could do,
Last night your little sleepover, showed me just how much,
You really do need your own yard to play with all your stuff,
Then we went around to Fraser's and watched the game together,
I doted on you every moment, wishing it would last forever,
He jumped and yelled it scared us both, but I soothed you back to calm,
You growled at him so I moved you close, to settle in my arms,
When I finally had you to myself, that night when we got home,
I couldn't keep my hands off you, it was so nice to have you alone,
I made a special bed for you, but knew you'd snuggle with me,
You've been like that since the very start, always under my sheets,
I was blessed to have ever met you, and blessed that you're still here,
I've written you so many poems, every one of them brings a tear,
The best part of our situation, is that you didn't go that far,
You're across the road, and for that each day, I thank my lucky stars,
It was hard enough to give you up, let alone never see you again,
It was through you I now understand why we call you man's best friend…

NEVER A MOMENT WITHOUT YOU

There's never a moment without you
I think of you all the time,
Such a beautiful little creature
Who stole this heart of mine,
Every moment you are in my thoughts
Not a single day goes by,
This tiny black beauty I love and taught
Still brings a tear to my eye,
I chat away as if you were here
The gibberish talk that I speak,
Pretending you are in my arms
And watching you fall asleep,
I know these moments are easing
Becoming less as time goes on,
So I spend these moments just dreaming
You're still here where you belong,
But I won't take you from your family
I won't ask them to give you up,
Your needs are met and they love you
I won't intrude or even disrupt,
Only distance stands between us
The memories we made I'll always treasure,
I love you so much, you gorgeous wee thing
You'll be in my heart forever…

27   LITTLE WHITE LAPIN

The Little White Lapin has a strange name indeed,
But it just so happens they're quite a popular breed,
They appear cute and hairy, but their incisors are sharp,
They can be quite scary, their razor claws lightning fast,
This rather small creature, in snow covered white,
Has flesh that's quite tender, if it's done and cooked right,
Their meat can be stewed and made into a pie,
In flaky puff pastry and baked for a while,
These little wee creatures are a great delicacy,
Maybe not in New Zealand, but they are overseas,
You see this white furry bunny has very lean meat,
And its ears long and funny for a delicious dog treat,
Their urine contains high levels of nitrogen,
It's like feeding your lawn an overdose of vitamins,
The waste from these rabbits, although the smelliest bit,
Is an organic fertiliser that is made from their shit,
Crush into a powder, grind with pestle and mortar,
Sprinkle over of your plants, then simply add water,
New Zealand is slow and missing out on this market,
Europe and China both know and rolled out the red carpet,
These countries discovered that every part of these creatures,
Is money uncovered with meat being the main feature,
Have you ever considered or maybe wanted to try,
The leanest of meats from shops you can't buy,
I know an old couple who have the most perfect place,
And they both recommend tasty rabbit back steaks,

So I tried it myself and you know daughters don't lie,
There's some on my fridge shelf that I add to stir fries,
Their flesh is real white and is highly nutritious,
It's very tasty and light, flavoursome and delicious,
Being quite the good builder Dad made a rabbitry,
He cares for them well and has plenty to breed,
That doesn't take long as we know rabbits breed fast,
Sometimes buck gets it wrong, confuses her front from her arse,
So Dad stands back and lends the buck some instruction,
For he gets carried away and tends to just rush in,
And then there's the does, who can be quite temperamental,
Sometimes they turn up their nose and refuse being parental,
She scratches and bounces and runs 'round the cage,
She bites and announces in a circling rampage,
Do not jump on me, you big white hairy buck,
I know our job is to breed, but you can go and get stuffed,
But when he finally succeeds their baby kits are so cute,
That's when buck has worked out, which end to root,
They're bred to be eaten, as I've said and described,
Their flesh is the leanest, but only the strongest survive,
They are the whole package, from the tip to their toe,
Every part of them used, but we're all too disposed,
To eat sheep and cows, 'cause that's what we've been told,
If Kiwi's knew how, they're worth their whole weight in gold,
Renowned the world over as an expensive white meat,
These White Lapin rabbits simply cannot be beat…

28   ALL ABOUT THE MEAT

How many types of meat do you like,

Do you stick to the same ones every night,

If I was to list kinds of meat for our food,

You'd see all the different things we can do,

The list is extensive, but I'll give it a go,

If I've missed any out, just let me know,

There's rump, sirloin and a nice piece of scotch,

These big pricey steaks are really top notch,

Pork belly, bacon and delicious rib eye,

But my personal favourite is a good silverside,

There's knuckle, brisket and shin on the bone,

These stewing meats just cook on their own,

Short ribs, porterhouse and even oxtail,

I tend to just buy whatever's on sale,

And what about good old fashioned lambs fry,

With a piece of schnitzel or a tender topside,

Is this the whole list, have I missed any out,

There's so many cuts that just come from a cow,

Like T-bone, neck chops and a cheeky beef stew,

Let alone the dozens of other meats too,

I recently learned a thing called sweet bread,

I wasn't quite sure if they were what they said,

Those big mountain oysters had me quite stumped,

Not for me sunshine, I'll just stick to the rump,

What's it like eating balls from big burly bulls,

Sitting down to a plate of cooked family jewels,

Perhaps one day I might give them a go,

For swallowing balls is something I'm yet to know,

But let's not forget the finest of dining,

Is to consume an animal's stomach lining,

Is this something that people actually like,

Enjoying the taste of a big bowl of tripe,

Chuck in some garlic, onions and herbs,

I have to admit this is thee most absurd,

Getting back to the topic of meat a-gain,

Another strange food people like is sheep's brains,

Now there's an image that just tops the lot,

That wrinkled up mess will likely give you the trots,

I can honestly say I'll give that one a pass,

Be it balls or brains, I'll just stick to the arse,

A nice tender butt is all that I need,

Not that strange other stuff on a plate for my tea,

There's so many choices and ways to cook meat,

Whatever your choice, it's bon appètit…

29   IT'S A BUTCHER'S LIFE

Each day that breaks in the early morn,

He slowly wakes to rise at dawn,

Dons his apron and cold white boots,

He hears the driver give a little toot,

The boys chip in to unload the goods,

Some local lads from the neighbourhood,

His cold hands welcome the warm sunrise,

"Ahhh," he says, "it's a butcher's life."

He brews a cuppa fit for one,

And feels the warmth of the rising sun,

Makes his way through the plastic curtains,

Checks the chiller to see she's workin',

She's loaded up, but not for long,

By the end of the day it'll all be gone,

Eager customers pull in the drive,

"Ahhh," he says, "it's a butcher's life."

Opens the shop as they make their way,

In to collect the orders they made,

Cows and sheep and pigs galore,

One by one they exit the door,

All wrapped up and neatly packed,

These cuts of meat that were on the racks,

That familiar sound as more people arrive,

"Ahhh," he says, "it's a butcher's life."

The midday sun now beating down,
He gets a break from the bustling crowd,
As they slowly empty out his store,
He makes his way through the chiller door,
Gets a strip of smoky bacon,
To satisfy his belly achin',
There's little time to grab a bite,
"Ahhh," he says, "it's a butcher's life."
Tools and equipment are used for meat,
Like trimming, cutting and curing beef,
He takes his time to ensure it's right,
And cuts every piece the perfect size,
There's many skills a butcher needs,
In many towns they're a dying breed,
As he sharpens up his boning knife,
"Ahhh," he says, "it's a butcher's life."
The sun soon settles upon the day,
As the butcher puts his tools away,
There's so much cleaning to be done,
As he watches the setting of the sun,
Many hours go into a hard day's work,
The days are long, but he knows his worth,
For customers come from far and wide,
To his little shop in the countryside,
He closes up and breathes a gentle sigh,
"Ahhh," he says, "this is the life"...

30   FIGHT TO THE DEATH

There's much to do in the working week,

Make many a sausage from pork or beef,

But if the shop is closed just after lunch,

Everyone knows he's gone out to hunt,

Just him in the bush absorbed by trees,

And his musty scent carried on the breeze,

Deep in the woods he hears a snort,

The cry of an angry warning call,

"I'm stronger than you with my mighty tusks,

Step into view if you really must,

There's many a man that's come in here,

You may be strong, but I smell your fear,

Are you going to be my match today,

You certainly won't if I have my way,

I'll pound the earth and prepare for war,

My unbridled worth is what you're hunting for,"

But the brazen hunter stayed out of view,

And prepared himself for what will ensue,

A fight to the death between man and boar,

Neither will rest till blood spills no more,

Deep in the scrub he sets a trap,

With a ferocious tug he let it snap,

The boar came rushing to this almighty sound,

And shook the earth as he hit the ground,

From behind the bushes the hunter appeared,

His heart was pounding, but he showed no fear,

Leaping forward with his steely knife,

Drove it into the neck with a single strike,

There was only this moment, one chance left,

To ensure that boar lay to his rest,

The hunter stood tall, with a deadly blow,

He drove that knife deep till the blood had slowed,

The boar knew then he had met his match,

As the hunter returned with his mighty catch,

Placing his foot upon his bloodied prize,

Gallant and triumphant was the look in his eyes,

"Over the years you've met men like me,

But none so brave as what you've just seen,

I wrestled with you with just my knife,

Valiantly withdrew your tremendous life,

'Twas a glorious victory between man and boar,

Remembered in history with your tusks on my wall"...

I LOVE A GOOD SAUSAGE

I love a good sausage in the morning, taste the juices on my lips,

Big and round, feel it going down, it's the perfect morning kiss,

You can have your eggs and bacon, if that is what you wish,

But a nice warm long hard sausage, is my favourite breakfast dish,

It can't be any old sausage, it must be from Mokau,

I love the taste of Bryan's sausage as I feel it going down,

He whips one up especially, with a drizzle of some maple,

The sausage Bryan gives me has become my morning staple,

I love his porky flavour, but I much prefer his beef,

The juice I like to savour is the drizzle he makes so sweet,

I can taste it in his sausage when I put it in my mouth,

The things he does in that back room makes my taste buds spin around,

He has quite a reputation, for his sausage is well known,

I drive for many hours to have his sausage for my own,

He wraps it up so nicely, especially for me,

Bryan's handmade sausage is the juiciest indeed,

People come from far and wide to this little Mokau town,

Can't resist the taste of Bryan's meaty sausage in their mouth,

I know I'm not the only one, who's willing and held hostage,

For many women have succumbed to wanting Bryan's sausage…

KIWI TUCKER

Where can you go to get great Kiwi tucker,
A meal that's as good as one from your mother,
Look no further if you must have the best,
A small seaside town has heard your request,
It has all you desire, but this food truck is seasonal,
Feel free to enquire, their prices are reasonable,
Burgers for kids without all the salad,
Omelettes of whitebait for those with soft palates,
Chicken kebabs or a hearty steak meal,
Sausage on bread, get two for a deal,
There's Surf and Turf that comes with the lot,
That's my favourite burger at this summertime spot,
I jump in the car with a few of my mates,
But the All Day Brekky is what they feed their face,
Sausages, bacon, eggs and hash browns,
And a thermos of coffee to wash it all down,
I'm still yet to try the Mighty Mokau,
I've heard it's the best tasting burger around,
So whether you're local or just passing through,
Come check out their menu and taste this great food,
It's prepared and then cooked in a food caravan,
And served to your table by the most handsome man,
And his staff of real friendly, beautiful girls,
It's the best Kiwi tucker in the whole bloody world…

33   MAGNIFICENT MOKAU

With stunning natural scenery and the most tranquil atmosphere,

This beautiful remote seaside town is spectacular any time of year,

It's not overrun with oodles of shops, just a handful or so in town,

It's the perfect, quaint, little place to stop, for there's very few people around,

At the mouth of the Mokau River, there's so much here you can do,

Come away feeling invigored, be absorbed by the breathtaking views,

Go for a stroll on the glorious beach, walk miles on the deserted shore,

Skinny dip in the big blue sea, there's so much here to explore,

Just north of the New Plymouth district, situated on the west coast,

Bring the kids and pack them a picnic, hitch the trailer and bring your boat,

On a nice, warm, sunny day, when skies are clear and all cloud free,

Jump in the car and make your way, fly a kite on the shores of the sea,

You don't need a lot of dough, just a full tank and a free weekend,

Come see how Mokau grows, when there's whitebait stands to attend,

You'll see quite a sudden influx, as the owners all rush into town,

All sitting in their handmade huts, it's the busiest place around,

Whitebait season is a two month slot, and boy does Mokau boom,

You'd be lucky to find a camping spot, but the Awakino might have some room,

It's the local pub just up the road, with food and beers for sale,

Built a hundred and ten odd years ago, it boasts New Zealand's finest ales,

I have a good friend who lives here, has been for thirty five years,

At the top of the really big hill, accessible in only first gear,

He hunts and fishes for all his grub, and completely lives off grid,

His land backs onto native scrub, such an envious life he lives,

The city folk he left behind, to surround himself in this world,

Not interested in the nine to five, just him, the bush and his girls,

If I was awake thirty years ago, I, too, would have bought some land,

Filled it with trees I wanted to grow, walk the beach barefoot on the sand,

But alas, I've always lived in the city, but I long for this peaceful life,

To spend my days in a garden made pretty, and sleep under stars at night,

When I visit Laurence on top of the hill, life feels so much better,

Magnificent Mokau is so tranquil, I wish I could stay forever…

BECAUSE OF YOU

I was lost before without you, I could feel it in my bones,

Wandering about the place, trying to find my way back home,

You helped me see and brought about a different point of view,

Everything that's happened, was all because of you,

I thought I didn't need you, but I see now that I do,

The drive I have and the love I feel was something I never knew,

It was just my job that brought me down, not life here at the zoo,

Now I wake to brighter mornings and my sky is always blue,

Sometimes it's very difficult, to see we're in a rut,

Can't see the forest through the trees, but you know that you are stuck,

A simple change to a better job was all it really took,

To readjust my thoughts again and focus on my book,

I welcome this new distraction and what it's offered me,

Get my thoughts back on track and be the person I want to be,

I know you'll never leave my side and I too won't ever leave yours,

You've loved me every day of my life, I could never close that door,

No longer lost, I found myself, I can feel it in my bones,

Through your endless love and guidance, I found my way back home…

35   LITTLE BOY, BIG HEART

"I'm all big now Mummy," he said with a gleam in his eye,

Holding my hand for balance, he takes it all in his stride,

One, two, three, jump, over the puddles he goes,

Life is yet to reveal itself and that day he's yet to know,

Too small for big activities, I feel his grip tighten,

But nothing sways his adventurous ways, and of this I am frightened,

What will come of my youngest son as he grows into a man,

To him right now life is full of fun, but one day he'll understand,

His struggle to achieve what others can as he strives to get ahead,

The adaptations he will need to hold him in good stead,

He has much to learn about limitations, in a world that's built on money,

Is my job to lower expectations, or just simply be his mummy,

Climbing onto the monkey bars, he swings with all his might,

The big heart in him will slowly wear thin, when he learns he has to fight,

By using his mouth, not his fists, as he discovers the power of words,

I catch his eye and blow him a kiss, and pray his voice will be heard,

I remember the moment so vividly, he got knocked to the ground,

My legs took off underneath me, my screams a silent sound,

They came 'round the corner not braking, and blindly ran him over,

I could feel my whole body shaking, the driver was far from sober,

Attempting to get off the monkey bars, he calls to me for help,

I rush to his side in the nick of time, as he slowly steadies himself,

"Mummy, it's fallen off again, can we get one that will stay?"

"Yes darling, I'm working on it, I just need a few more pays,"

I've been saying that for two whole years, but new legs don't come cheap,

As I wipe away his falling tears, I'm saving hard every week,

My little boy is so patient, and his heart is made of gold,

He spends his days just waitin', for that moment to be told,

I can afford the leg you need, one that won't fall off,

So you can run and jump with ease, till then I'll never stop,

As he puts himself back together, we head over to our picnic,

This routine he'll do forever, and get used to many a witness,

Ooh that boy has only one leg, I wonder how that occurred,

I can read the curious thoughts in their heads, and feel my insides stir,

I want to hold the driver accountable, but He said otherwise,

His actions were deplorable yes, but he did pay with his life,

His stupidity caused his death, those drunken thoughts in his head,

That decision he made has now left, a memory I relive with much dread,

I see my son smiling up at me, as I watch him enjoy his lunch,

Under the shade, we feel the breeze, but reality he's yet to confront,

As time went by, the less I cried, and the more I held his hand,

Every step of the way, every single day, I helped him become a man,

He would say to me, it's okay to be, a boy with just one leg,

I love you Mummy, despite no money, I remember what you said,

Life is cruel, but we're given tools and always have a choice,

You gave to me, the love I need and that became my voice,

"I'm all big now," he said to the crowd, that gathered to hear his words,

The gleam in his eye, never left his side, his philosophies widely heard,

Of all the teachers I had in my life, none were as wise as my son,

Blessed to have him by my side, he taught me at an age so young,

Yes life is hard and can be cruel, but you must please understand,

It was your love that got me through, and made me into a man,

Our disabilities don't define us, they're just something that we have,

No existence is ever perfect, live with it, happy or sad,

He chose the path of acceptance and his smile will always shine,

Through all of life's deceptions, he's been grateful for his time,

I have two legs and always have, but never did I see,

The strength I drew from my young lad, and the love he gave to me,

Through thick and thin, with each small win, every battle that he fought,

I learned from him, to never give in, you only have to change your thoughts…

MICHAEL

I'm glad you're here to talk to me and remind me the beauty of life,

So easily you could've been taken, like on that fateful night,

In fact you've had more than one, I think the count is three,

Misjudged or underestimated, either way you're here with me,

I may not see you very often, but your voice I long to hear,

It's always nice to speak to you and be a listening ear,

When you call me up to talk, I drop everything I do,

Nothing ever gets in the way when I am talking to you,

I know that we live miles apart, but I'm only a phone call away,

Just know you're always in my heart, every single day,

There are pictures of you on my wall that I like to look at often,

Photos of you big and small, my heart just melts and softens,

There's nothing in this world to me that's more important than you,

You've always made me so happy in everything you do,

You inspired me to write this book and take a leap of faith,

That people may just want to look and my poems aren't a waste,

They're what I do and have always done, I write my thoughts in ink,

Been rhyming words since I was young, rhyming everything I think,

As I write this poem just for you and put the words together,

I just want it always to be known, you're my number one forever...

MY HEART

You stole something from me, a long time ago,

I hadn't even met you, but how could I say no,

Your innocence and purity, I simply couldn't resist,

You came into my life and what you stole I do not miss,

You took it unbeknown to either you or me,

Ever since that day you've swept me off my feet,

You never gave it back nor would I ever ask,

What you stole from me was the essence of my heart,

The love I have for you is unlike any other,

The richest love of all comes from being your mother,

I knew you before you were born, I felt you in my womb,

The radiant glow you gave me, brighter than any moon,

The love that grew inside me, deep down in my soul,

I simply gave you life and with it my heart you stole,

The world I brought you into can be a barren place,

But you have all my love to keep your smiling face,

You'll always be special to me no matter how old you are,

I just want to say I love you from the bottom of my heart…

LOVE IS A BONUS

Life is a gift, what does that mean,

I ponder this concept and imagine a dream,

Soaring the skies and exploring new realms,

Soaring so high to new depths I delve,

A flight like no other, I sail on through,

New heights I discover together with you,

Words can't describe something like this,

Each moment so precious, that's why life is a gift,

Many sliding door moments I did not explore,

Was it all meant to be, whatever's in store,

I can only but wonder the beauty that is,

The life that we have and to others we give,

I care and I love and to my surprise,

To share all I have truly opened my eyes,

So if life is a gift and I share all I do,

Then my love is a bonus and I give mine to you…

NEXT HIT SONG

Putting a melody to my rhymes,

Tempo and tones in every line,

How is this done, does anyone know,

I could write all the lyrics and start off slow,

Come up with a beat from a couple of sticks,

Humming a tune might do the trick,

If only I knew how to put my words,

Into a song and get them heard,

Then maybe my poems could possibly be,

The next hit song from a poet like me,

But alas, I cannot so I need some help,

And work with someone just like myself,

An artist to show me where tunes belong,

And turn all my poems into a song…

40   GREEN EYES

It lives deep inside me, no one can see, its dangers only apparent to me,
Quietly sleeping, no one's in sight, keep peaceful this beast and its nasty bite,
With emerald green and tinge of red, it'll open its eyes at the first word said,
Laughs with me with my friends around, my lovers though, they disturb its ground,
Once it is out I cannot contain, it swallows me whole and causes me pain,
It warns me first, but soon explodes, wipes out all who gets in its road,
It's lived inside me all of my life, it's there when I wake morning or night,
I've asked it to leave or remain asleep, explained the hurt and countless grief,
It hinders my thoughts and my lover's too, it drives them away till I'm left with you,
I've tried to learn how to get along, with my darkest friend who does me wrong,
What lurks within me, can you guess, my green eyed monster will never rest,
But I think it's time you left me now, it's time for you to go,
You've lingered 'round me long enough, hiding in the shadows,
I've always known the sinister, nasty streak you have,
For many years you broke my heart, to be rid of you I'm glad,
So I bid good riddance to you old friend, I'm making a brand new start,
There's someone here to challenge you, so best that we now part,
I won't miss you when you're gone, I don't want you in my life,
All the sorrow you have brought has caused me endless strife,
So leave me now and don't come back, today is where it ends,
I've had enough, I wave goodbye to my jealous green eyed friend…

41   A CHANCE ENCOUNTER

A chance encounter with a handsome young man,
She searched through her phone till his name was at hand,
Maybe this person was someone she thought,
But to her surprise an unknown was sort,
The daring young lady asked his request,
So the handsome young man indulged her behest,
A spark had ignited and fluttered her heart,
This was not the man she thought from the start,
A stranger he was, but unknown to she,
What lay in wait she could hardly believe,
Rugged, ripped, tanned and tall,
The handsome young stranger answered her call,
"Will you see me my sweetness, may I be so bold,
Your alluring beauty and long locks of gold,"
Blushing at his brazen advance she replied,
This gorgeous young woman just could not deny,
How besotted and smitten she had quickly become,
By this chance encounter with a stranger handsome,
As the days slowly passed their romance had bloomed,
When the handsome young stranger entered her room,
Seeing before him, her sparkling green eyes,
The undressed beauty called out in surprise,
"I've been waiting for you, many dreams in my head,

As I lay down gently at night in your bed,"

Her soft pale skin aroused him so much,

He longed for more of her delicate touch,

Entwined as one, between sheets so white,

He caressed her soft skin all through the night,

Not wanting a single moment to end,

The handsome young stranger called out again,

"My desire for you has awoken in me,

Your kiss so tender, my heart skips a beat,"

The beauty beside him yearns his romance,

Her lust is so strong, she jumps at the chance,

Seduced by the handsome young stranger's charms,

She gently lays herself in his arms,

Their passion surreal, sublime and so raw,

Burning like fire, they both longed for more,

Caressing and kissing till morning sunrise,

The smitten young woman stared into his eyes,

"My desire for you has awoken in me,

This beautiful stranger that I longed to see,"

Pressing his lips so gently on hers,

They whispered sweet nothings, but neither one heard,

The sound from two strangers who captured each heart,

No longer just strangers who walk their own path…

42   MISTY BLUE

Green or blue, mysterious and new, what lay behind those beautiful eyes,

Intrigued, I was captured, what was I to do, was there something between her and I,

Not one to intrude, but I had to pursue, this woman had caught my attention,

I couldn't let go, I just had to know, was I labouring under a misapprehension,

Did she feel the same, shall I call out her name, as my heart skipped a few beats,

In a moments embrace, I kissed her soft face, I shall sweep her off of her feet,

With long golden hair, and her skin so fair, I melted into her arms,

She's all that I dreamed, nothing more do I need, I'm spellbound by her charms,

Then thoughts in my head, over things left unsaid, but I really wanted to say,

Would you like to be, with a man like me, in my arms forever you'd stay,

I'd give you the world, if you'd be my girl, but I lacked the courage to ask,

Will she just find another, to kiss and love her, I fear that I may miss my chance,

So with brazen approach, from the words I just spoke, bravely uttered from my lips,

"Would my lady of beauty, give herself to me, are you besotted by true love's first kiss?"

As I called out her name, of my maiden fair dame, she turned to me in surprise,

"Yes my sweet one, it is you that I love," and she drew me in with those eyes,

With her skin so fair, and her long golden hair, in awe, I was then hypnotised,

How could such a beauty, do these things to me, leave me stunned and mesmerised,

For all that I asked, would soon come to pass, if my lady would be by my side,

As we walked arm in arm, her soft tender palms, touched the side of my face,

I turned to my beauty, pulled her into me, and gently closed our embrace,

Warmly I glanced, as she gracefully danced, by the moonlight of a darkened sky,

Then thoughts in my head, dreamed of us newly wed, she would be the most beautiful bride,

She held out her hand, "come with me, handsome man, and be with me romantically,"

Laying down on the bed, as she sweetly said, "make love to me passionately,"

There was no one other, for my beautiful lover, only me to kiss her soft hands,

"It's always been you, from that moment I knew, and saw the most handsome man,

All that you asked, has now come to pass, I choose to be by your side,

You're all that I dreamed, nothing more do I need, I want you for the rest of my life"...

43   GENTLE FRIEND

If we were on a deserted island with no one else around,
No influence or any opinions to run us into the ground,
Judging me for who I am or judging you for liking me,
Just two people on the island, seeing what we see,
I would walk straight over to you because what I see so far,
Is a gentle giant who noticed me from the other side of the bar,
Your rugged looks and bushmen gear, yet so quietly spoken,
I must admit I was intrigued, my curiosity awoken,
Who is this man all rough and tough, I've not seen him before,
Whoever you are, you got my attention, maybe I should find out more,
So I went outside, and sat beside, this man with tattooed arms,
Just like I thought, he's a gentle sort, ruffled looks with a sense of calm,
His drinking mates, moved about the place, but unbeknown to them,
I could see through the exterior of their gentle giant friend,
There is no art upon my body, no ink of any kind,
Just some scars from my battle wounds, but I keep those out of sight,
I'm a little shy and quite reserved, some days I keep to myself,
I do my best to hide and preserve my flaws from anyone else,
You didn't know the day we met that I have no tattoos,
That's not to say I cannot like someone who's covered like you,
So here we are, from across the bar, exchanging hidden glances,
But I'm too shy, to ask you why, it's with me you're taking chances,
So here's my number anyway, perhaps one day you'll text,
And I'll see inside the guy outside, the gentle giant that I met...

44   TWO NINETY NINE

The item was actually two ninety nine, but I said the item was three,
Rounding it up to the nearest dollar didn't seem that important to me,
But you took it far too seriously and called me out on a lie,
Questioned my morals and ethics, to the point of saying goodbye,
This insignificant discrepancy does not sum up my world,
I'm everything I said I was, a kind hearted, loving girl,
I shared my intimate thoughts with you as well as my lonely heart,
I never imagined being punished like this, now I question who you are,
Can you honestly tell me you're the nicest guy, everything your profile said,
Or did you just say all that was needed to get me into bed,
Are you really the photo on my screen, are you bubbly and down to earth,
If we were to ever meet in person, are you handsome and truly diverse,
I find it somewhat amusing, but mostly just downright strange,
That someone who puts themselves out there, is on a completely different page,
So why bother with all the effort, of being on a dating site,
When something as little as one cent, makes you judge my entire life,
So let's take a minute, as I sum up, what all that really means,
Petty, pathetic and slightly eccentric, not my type of human being,
I should probably thank my lucky stars, that you showed me at the start,
You're not the nicest guy at all, I'm pleased I didn't give you my heart,
So I bid you goodbye and wish you success for that special someone to meet,
I know I'll fall in love someday, it's just a matter of them finding me…

45   WORLD OF DREAMS

The morning greeted me with a soft, cool breeze sweeping my naked skin,

I shivered gently as my mind wandered off with romantic thoughts of him,

The dark grey sky then caught my eye, as I looked upon the day,

My hopes it seems, are merely dreams, so I put my thoughts away,

What will come with the setting sun, when light soon turns to dark,

Does he know my feelings grow, every touch ignites a spark,

Can he read my mind and feel each time, my heart begins to race,

As he draws near can he sense the fear, that is written upon my face,

Caught between my heart and dreams, I find myself alone,

I drew the curtains and shut the door, closed my mind to the unknown,

The grey clouds above, like falling in love, drifts away on a gentle breeze,

And as I've aged, so have the days, and thunder is all I meet,

The rain then starts, and tears me apart, till I'm soaking wet and blue,

My naked skin, shivers within, but will warm to thoughts of you,

A tender touch is all I need, your loving arms to comfort me,

And gently place into my hand, a caring heart that understands,

How much I yearn for your embrace, warmth and love I can't escape,

My lips will try to tell you when, they dare to speak those words again,

The love from you I dream at night, in hope that you will share your life,

My mind has drifted off once more, with romantic thoughts of play,

Caress your neck and taste your lips, as I dreamily drift away,

Do I dare to think of you this much, love can be so blind,

Lay with you as you gently touch my skin, my heart, my mind,

Will grey clouds fall upon me soon, like they have done in the past,

Like wilting flowers shedding bloom, I shut away my heart,

The cool air morning invites me in, aroused by its steely breeze,

Piercing my cold, white, naked skin, allured to a world of dreams,

I shuddered in that moment, of what had gone before,

I left my heart wide open, then felt the slamming of the door,

But this time I won't escape, love I feel in each rain drop,

I won't make the same mistake, my past troubles can be forgot…

IF I COULD FIND A MAN

If only I could find a man that loved me true for all I am,
Not someone bigger or someone small
not someone richer who has it all,
Just the way I am like this, an attractive woman with a passionate kiss,
Then I would give my heart to thee and love him for all of eternity,
Not for his penis or wallet size, just who he is and what's inside,
Tonight I saw a couple in love, but people said he had an ugly mug,
She was stunning, hair dark and long, in her eyes his looks weren't wrong,
Head held high regarding myself, but before I know it he's with someone else,
All it takes is a pretty skirt and soon enough I'm of little worth,
Traded up or traded in, that's how my love life has always been,
If only I could find a man that loves me for everything I am,
I would show this guy a beautiful world,
the love he desires from a sensual girl,
I'd lavish him with endless affection, if only I could hold his attention,
Not watch his heart soon wander off,
to some short skirt who struts her stuff,
I want to be the only one that rocks his world and shows him love,
I dream of meeting this man someday and fall in love along the way,
Hold him in my arms so tight
and be with him for the rest of my life…

IF I COULD FIND A WOMAN

If only I could find a woman,

who cooked and cleaned and was really good looking,

She'd give me a job at dawn's first light,

after making love all through the night,

I'd lavish her with diamond rings, a brand new car and a house to clean,

Have beautiful children and live in the woods,

to find this woman if only I could,

But the ones I meet are superficial, demanding it all till my account is crippled,

I've been on sites looking for love,

but their faces don't match their profile above,

So I went to some bars in a few busy towns, but none of the women wanted me around,

Some did for the night, but held out their palm,

emptied my wallet and chewed off their arm,

So looks it seems is what they like, not really interested in what's inside,

If only I could find a lady,

who likes a picnic under a tree that's shady,

I would kiss her gently and hold her hand,

I would be the most romantic man,

Lay down a rug for my one sweet love,

and dreamily stare at the sky above,

I'd provide for her the best of things, cherish and treasure the love she brings,

To this lonely heart she would have and hold,

together forever until we grew old…

48   IF ONLY LOVE COULD BE FOUND

The lonely love story of finding someone, can be a disheartening task,

If people just realised all it takes is putting someone first, not last,

A man sees love through his manly eyes and a woman sees love through hers,

The reality is they both want the same thing, in finding a love they deserve,

It's something innate to all human beings, to be cared for and adored,

But the needs of one taking over the romance, just leads to heartache ignored,

Love is a feeling within our hearts that requires the greatest devotion,

It's not something you trade or buy on sale, it's the deepest of all our emotions,

Similar to a flowing river, it's not a bargaining tool from receiver to giver,

Love is about complete acceptance, for who they are and what they need,

It is not about looks, or who cleans and cooks, about money or material greed,

But only when you give love first, you will see how it flows back to you,

Because love doesn't know any boundaries, when it's pure, real and true,

The man and the woman in the story above are keeping themselves at bay,

She must be this and he must be that, but love doesn't work that way,

They're seeing love as a commodity, that can be given to us if we ask,

But love is a feeling that cannot be seen, as it only resides in our hearts,

So consider this next time you're out looking, for that special person somewhere,

Love will find you first and foremost, if your heart is willing to share…

49   THREE'S A CROWD

I can't believe you phoned me up just to tell me how to live,

Your mate apparently likes me, so to him my love I should give,

Sorry sweet cheeks, but you've got it wrong, there's things that I must do,

And being tied down for somebody's love, is not for me like it is for you,

I'm such a free spirit and enjoy my time, spent wherever I choose to be,

Come and go to the people I know, enjoying my life just being me,

But I can relate to your point of view and completely understand,

How you think we're so good together that your mate should be my man,

But I'm not one for relationships, all they've done is hold me back,

I want to explore so much more, find opportunities and just relax,

I am who I am and make a good friend, but tied down is not for me,

I have my plan, in my travelling van and remaining forever carefree,

But thank you for the pep talk, now I have a question for you,

If I was to date, your best of mates, would you constantly be there too,

Would it be a private relationship, just between him and I,

Or would there always be, a circle of three, and I'd get pushed to the side,

I've seen this many times before, where mates influence their control,

And sure enough, time and again, it's to you their partner consoles,

Every time there is an up or down, it's discussed with the best mate first,

This creates the biggest mistake and makes the relationship worse,

I'm a very private person and dislike my life on display,

I need to know the things I say, aren't shared in any way,

We know it's plainly obvious, you two are quite good mates,

But three's a crowd so there is no point, me even trying to instigate,

It never works with any third wheel, so I'll tell you both again,

I'm not into a relationship, but I'll be his bloody good friend…

50   YOURS AS YOU WISH

Did I push you away by saying no, is that something I'll live to regret,

Should I have held your hand and pulled you close, and welcomed you into my bed,

You thought of this moment many times, but for me it was the first,

Like a delicate bombshell in your mind, you released on me when it burst,

Now this burden you no longer carry, you shifted most of its weight,

Unknowingly onto my shoulders, disconcertion was left in its wake,

Alone, confused and concerned, it conjured up many a question,

With answers I may never learn, I'm left perplexed by the suggestion,

I never thought of being with you, in that kind of romantic way,

But it wasn't romance you were looking for, just a part that I play,

How far down this road had you ventured, was this going to be the one time,

Or did you plan on it being repeated, and continue for many a night,

Were there going to be several positions, or just a simple perfunctory act,

Would you snuggle with me and give kisses, or roll over and turn your back,

With no one to share your burden and off load your troubles to,

You thought I could heal years of hurtin', allowing what you wanted to do,

Drowning in much apprehension, from the courage it must have taken,

You found it hard to even mention, I could see your whole body shakin',

The risk you took to tell me and the risk I took to listen,

Like a tidal wave fell on me, smothered by love so smitten,

But you knew I already loved you, I just couldn't accept your request,

A moment I'll always remember and those words I'll never forget,

What had you planned for the morning, would I be cooking you bacon and eggs,

All this occurred without warning, an awkwardness we would both dread,

Or would we have really enjoyed it and wished it had happened before,

Not waited so long for this moment, experiencing what you longed to explore,

All I have now are just questions, because I chose to turn you down,

Be it a right or wrong suggestion, you then chose not to stick around,

Maybe one day if I'm ready, I could give you the love you need,

When my thoughts are calm and steady, I'll be yours as you wish and please...

51   JUST CALL ME

If I stopped calling you, how long would it take,

Before you called me, do you like that I wait,

With anticipation that one day you'll call,

Sometimes it feels you don't want to at all,

You poured out your heart and told me no lies,

I'm left torn apart with tears in my eyes,

I go over that night and the things that you said,

Replaying those words over again in my head,

There was no right answer, only truth that I thought,

Being honest and true, but disappointment it brought,

Is that why you're quiet, do you prefer that I go,

The truth in that question I may never know,

A brave face you sport, but your feelings inside,

Reveal something deeper you just hide behind,

Is patience a virtue, you'll force I possess,

Or is this us parting, you prefer I forget,

Which ever it is, can you please tell me true,

I just need to know so I can move on from you,

Time seems to linger when I stare at the clock,

Each day I grow weaker, like life has just stopped,

Paused in that moment when you spoke to me,

Telling me something in your eyes I could see,

How much you were hurting, but happy as well,

Please don't desert me, you know I won't tell,

I love you so much and it kills me inside,

To think that you've gone away just to hide,

There's no need to run from me or now this,

If that's what you want then I'll respect your wish,

Just know that I'm here and will always be,

Waiting for you when you're ready for me,

I gave you my heart the day we first met,

A magical moment I will never forget,

I don't want it back, it's yours to keep safe,

Just call me sometime and put a smile on my face…

52   MISTER SHOES

It was one damn thirty when I woke to the sound,
And for two more hours you played it loud,
All I heard was boom boom boom,
As far away as I am in my room,
I looked out the window and saw it was you,
Our noisiest neighbour it was mister shoes,
So I put ear plugs in and then tried to sleep,
Each night this happens week after week,
But to no avail, so I knocked on your door,
Told you nicely I can't take anymore,
Please turn it down I'm trying to snooze,
When you opened the door I could smell all the booze,
A party for one can be fun if you like,
But not that damn loud in the middle of the night,
Twenty more minutes before it finally stopped,
The music had ended, at long last it was off,
The sound of peace was then restored,
As I grumbled my way back to my door,
Mister shoes should consider what time of day,
He chooses his music that loud to play,
To wake up his neighbours in the wee hours,
Just makes people grumpy, shitty and sour,
I like music too, I play electric guitar,
But not that damn loud you can hear it that far,
So I ask you again, just one last time,
Play your sounds softly and then you'll be fine,
We all have to live here and work together,
Be mindful of others today and forever…

53   FREEDOM TO MOVE

I'd love to just travel and go where I like,

Not be stuck in a building for all of my life,

The freedom to move is freedom to live,

I'll take from myself all I can give,

I won't be caged nor a job clip my wings,

Just reach for the sky, explore new things,

I saw the light and I broke the chains,

I lived in the dark, but never again,

I know what I want, I know what to do,

One step at a time was all that I knew,

Failed my way to each little success,

Determined to always do my best,

I am not my job, don't need a career,

I won't work for some twit year after year,

My focus was on purely just me,

What I discovered then set me free,

I am today what I dreamed and saw,

I took the plunge and yearned for more,

My life became all that I chose,

Had no direction, just followed my nose,

From scribbled on notes, the starting phase,

Designed a logo and bought a name,

So what made all this come to fruition,

It was one simple choice, an idea, a decision…

54   DRESSING IT UP

There's a handsome young man that lives down my street,
I walked past one day and saw the size of his meat,
He was dressing it up in all sorts of things,
I could see through the window, but he could not see me,
Next thing I know it was cupped in his hands,
He was getting it up as fast as he can,
Onto the bench where he proceeded to grease,
All of the sides of his very large meat,
He then turned it slowly so he could ensure,
There was plenty room left so he could fit more,
He moved it around to get the right angle,
Tucked it all in so nothing would dangle,
His big sweaty hands and reddened hot face,
I could smell through the window how nice it would taste,
What he did next was quite a surprise,
I could hardly believe my very own eyes,
He placed it in gently so it stayed nice and warm,
Turned up the heat and then closed the door,
With awe I gazed at his really large bone,
His meat was so tender it fell off on its own,
He then pulled it out to check the inside,
I gasped when I saw it was now half the size,
This isn't exactly what I had in mind,
But at least I can say I had a good time,
Watching a man carefully tend to his meat,
This handsome young man that lives down my street,
Who tenderly made the moment just right,
He can bring 'round his bone to me any night…

55   ONLY EYES FOR ME

Tender to the touch, warm and pink on the inside,

I feel a sudden rush, my need for you I cannot hide,

I don't have you every day, but when I do it's utter bliss,

I can never turn away from your taste upon my lips,

So succulent and tender, there's nothing quite like you,

The moment that you enter, arouses senses I never knew,

You're smaller than I'm used to, but size means nowt to me,

You're oh so appetising and guaranteed to please,

The few times that I've been with you has brought tremendous pleasure,

The enjoyment that I go through every time that we're together,

I can taste you on my lips before you've even touched my mouth,

My gaze is fixed upon you, mesmerised like I am now,

Just seeing you in front of me, knowing you are mine,

Feeling every part of you warming me inside,

There's really no comparison, it's you I like the most,

Nothing tastes as good as you, there's nothing that comes close,

Your juices linger on my tongue, I let nothing go to waste,

Savouring every mouthful of my scrumptious eye fillet steak…

GETTIN' JERKY

On a warm summer's evening by a full moon, my moment of pleasure had ended too soon,

Wrapped up so tightly was my recent purchase, I waited so long, every penny was worth it,

It's little and hard, long, thin and sweet, I just couldn't resist this most tasty treat,

I held it together for as long as I could, savoured the flavour, it tasted so good,

Sometimes I found it a bit hard to chew, but I think that's what you're supposed to do,

If you move it around in your mouth just right, I reckon you could make it last all night,

There are no instructions, just comes in a wrap, I sink my teeth in with no holding back,

Why is it so little, I can take so much more, do they come any bigger, why be so small,

My moment of pleasure had ended so quick, in just a few mouthfuls I finished the stick,

If I had have known I would've bought two, enjoyed more of this flavour and not end so soon,

Have you ever had something like this in your life, thought something would last all through the night,

Got all prepared and you think it's the bomb, to only find out it's not really that long,

Let me give you a little piece of advice, this thin, long, hard thing may be real nice,

But I strongly suggest you find a bigger one, before you wind up like me with none,

I'm not being funny or in any way quirky,

It's just a real pleasure munching down on beef jerky…

FIRST THING I DO

The first thing I do, is suck on you, every morning when I wake,

In the middle of the night, without any light, no hour is ever too late,

Slide you into my hand, no matter what brand, and into my mouth you go,

For just a few seconds, you release your venom, and the pleasure truly explodes,

The relief is intense, your strength is immense, and I'm completely satisfied,

I release my tight grip, for just a small bit, long enough to rest for a while,

I don't hesitate, I can no longer wait, I need you all over again,

I'm reaching for you, it's just what I do, I will suck on you till you end,

I don't sleep well, I go through hell, whenever you're out of my sight,

I like you with me, in my mouth tenderly, every day and all through the night,

There's two days left, before I'm bereft, and no more of your taste on my lips,

You won't live in my palm, or slide into my bra, or gently rest on my hips,

We've done this too long, in my mouth you belong, every morning when I wake,

How will I survive, without you by my side, having withdrawals over my vape…

58   BABY BLUES

Thank you for looking after me and giving me cuddles at night,

I'm back where I started and happy again, just living a quiet life,

My Mummy was lost, but didn't know how to manage her baby blues,

When you took me in, she kept it a secret and didn't disclose to you,

How wrong she was to let me go, didn't give me a chance to shine,

If it wasn't for you, she would never have known, once she had realised,

I will never be Louie, but that doesn't mean she can't love me as well,

Her heart needs to heal and I can help, but only time will tell,

In my short life of just twelve weeks, I know what I need to be,

A companion and mate, so she doesn't vape, and ceases so much drinking,

I too am like you, and wished she had seen, how good I was from day one,

You forgave her her folly and allowed her to see, she too needs someone to love,

If it wasn't for you helping her out, she would've quietly slipped away,

Kept to herself so no one would know, and just simply smiled through the pain,

So now you see, it wasn't just me, that you rescued taking me in,

You gave her the chance to mend her own heart, and be able to start again,

She knows I'm not Louie, I'm different, I'm Nui, but only thanks to you,

No matter my name, I'm loyal all the same, and appreciate you getting her through,

We both truly hope that you're really okay and don't have a heavy heart,

If it wasn't for you and her mistake to undo, she'd regret that we had to part,

We can't thank you enough for bringing me back and letting us be together,

She knows at times she's a hard nut to crack, but this time I'm hers forever…

59   SWEEPING STREETS

The writing was on the wall, but this time I made sure to read,

And be aware of the workplace bullying that was slowly happening to me,

I recognised all the signs because this has happened to me before,

But this time I was wise to their antics and promptly walked out the door,

I won't go to work to be deliberately hurt, by someone in a higher position,

I won't tolerate this from anyone, it's my prerogative to make that decision,

There's a piece of advice I heard long ago and it's held me in good stead,

"You've only one life, so don't let it go, just remember you're a long time dead,

And don't take for granted the person you are, and just give yourself away,

If you're happy sweeping streets then sweep them, be grateful you're alive every day,"

So I went back to the job I'm good at, the one that I love and know,

A place where everyone's welcome, a little place I call hospo,

All walks of life go in there, to meet and mingle every night,

A place where secrets you share, can change the course of your life,

So if you find you're in a dilemma and need some inspiration,

Remember the wise words above, because life won't send you an invitation…

60   ONE LAST PUFF

When you put a lighter in your mouth instead of your very own vape,

I think it's time to now give up and accept your awaited fate,

That this is simply habitual and something you just don't need,

But cessation isn't that easy and clearly has you on your knees,

So as you put this thing in your mouth and have just one more draw,

Mistakenly putting a lighter in has got to be the last straw,

But yet you keep on buying them and having 'one last puff',

So tell me then, Miss Full of Shit, when are you truly going to give up,

You've been a smoker for many years and stopped tailor-mades three times,

Excuse me if this brings you to tears, as you're going out of your mind,

A lighter for Pete's sake, instead of a vape, what more will you actually do,

You could phone for help, walk past the shelf, but you end up buying a new,

So don't give up, on your 'one last puff,' just keep starting again,

No matter how hard this is for you, one day it'll come to an end…

61   NOT THIS TIME

Not this time, never again, no more,

This time I'm changing the locks on the door,

I must keep them all out, but especially you,

I'm turning my back, it's over, we're through,

I don't care where you go, I don't care where you are,

I must do this alone, the proof's in my scars,

The life that I want does not include you,

You're no longer my master, it's over, we're through,

I know you'll be waiting for me to resign,

Give up my post like I have done each time,

But not this time, no not anymore,

I mean what I say right down to my core,

I will finish this one, see it through to the end,

But I will not replace you, I won't do this again,

When I wake in the morning and open my eyes,

I will see the same world without you in my life,

The sun will still shine upon each day that breaks,

And each one I'll enjoy without wanting to vape…

62   A FIRE OF TORMENT

I have to learn some lessons, some lessons I don't want to learn,

Feeling the weight of their burden as they slowly start to stir,

Beaten by all I've become, downtrodden by who I am,

Fighting against all odds, to break free if only I can,

A dream I dream of one day, that maybe I will be,

The very person I want, and end years of bad company,

Am I alone in life's little struggles, do others feel its pain,

A burning fire of torment, but the embers still remain,

I wander alone by daylight, gripped by the perils within,

Then crippled under the moonlight as it slowly draws me in,

Will I ever break free from the chains, of enduring endless torture,

Just like a fire uncontained, burning steel and melting mortar,

Consumed by strength and might, as I battle this alone,

A war that's waged each night, I must do this on my own,

Learning the ugly truth of a lesson never taught,

Like sifting through the ashes of a fire never fought,

It's all upon me now as I attempt to understand,

To know one's self so intimately and not give in to my demands,

Destroy the licence I gave myself so many years ago,

I would never have started any of this, if only I had known…

63   MAKING IT HOME

A smoker with nothing to smoke, a lover with nothing to love,

My hurt remains unspoke and disappears like clouds above,

This journey must be done alone, only I can see it achieved,

It's a long hard row to hoe, solitude is all that I need,

As life continues all around me, I will take this final step,

I'm a prisoner without any bars, just my mind to deal with the mess,

As the power of thoughts succeed me, I cannot succumb to these words,

Temptations are taken too easy, must ignore everything that I've heard,

No one can rescue a prisoner, that is trapped in their own mind,

Just focus on each day before you, it's simply a matter of time,

I've walked many long hard roads, but I was younger in those days,

Not burdened with so many loads, whereas now there's one foot in the grave,

No pity for me on my journey, I did this all to myself,

My longing and constant yearning to think I was something else,

But, today the battle is greatest, by tomorrow it starts to wane,

A war I'm waging within, there's no scars to show for my pain,

Anyone that's done what I'm doing, achieved the journey alone,

The secret behind their winning was the focus of making it home…

64   CLEANING WINDOWS

What a beautiful house and spectacular view, as I look around at all the cleaning to do,

Where do I start, I soon asked myself, skirting boards, windows, or the dusty top shelf,

How about I start to remove the cobwebs, and then I can take out those musty bunk beds,

Air them all out for three or four days, as I work on the kitchen and then make my way,

Into the lounge room, hallway and bedrooms, but firstly I must find a really tall broom,

To reach all the webs, I can feel my neck ache, so I went back to the kitchen to give it a break,

This room won't take long, it's clean and quite small, till I looked inside each cupboard and drawer,

Another big job now lay at my feet, at this bloody rate I'll be here all week,

So I finished the cobwebs and stayed in the kitchen, knowing what was involved to complete my mission,

Just stay in here and start with the pans, and after two days it was all spick and span,

I was quietly pleased to have finished that room, finally get off my knees and put down the broom,

I'll go work on the lounge room, there's not much in there, just a couch and TV, reading books and a chair,

When I started to move all the items around, I saw there was many a spot to wipe down,

The fireplace, bricks, and the tiles underneath, a handful of logs and the long mantlepiece,

As I was wiping away to make it all clean, I got up halfway and guess what I'd seen,

Tucked in the corners up high in the dark, were quite a few cobwebs I missed at the start,

So out came the broom for one last sweep, now all the cobwebs are finally defeat,

But look at the shelf full of dust once again, those damn bloody spiders are no cleaners' friend,

Dusting the ornaments that I gently moved, until every last item was cleaned in that room,

Wiped down all the paintings and inside the cabinet, I tried to leave some things, but it's just such a habit,

To wipe any area that I see isn't clean, I simply can't help it, I guess that's just me,

I then vacuumed the lounge room to finish it off, when I heard Michael saying it was now time to stop,

We'll come back tomorrow and put up those beds, I've bought you a drink, so I did as he said,

We sat on the deck and admired the view, as I sculled back a couple of tasty cold brews,

Tomorrow I'll tackle the hallway real quick, it's the most empty room, there'll be nothing to it,

Just a handful of doors with large wooden frames, but there was so much more and I couldn't refrain,

From doing the job I said I would do, so I polished that hallway back to brand new,

Including the hat stand and two rusty bowls, that hold the umbrellas on days wet and cold,

Even polished the ladder right up to the top, nothing else mattered so I just didn't stop,

Till every inch of that hallway was shiny and bright, then after that, I called it a night,

There's one room left, which includes an ensuite, that's five days straight I've worked this week,

Mikes was observing and watching me work, he truly agrees, every penny I'm worth,

So back the next morning with one room to go, the ensuite, the dusting and cleaning windows,

As well as the frames around all of the glass, another big job 'cause I'm such a short arse,

But thankfully Mikes had a ladder that's tall, reaching top panes was no problem at all,

Then I moved the great wardrobe and polished it up, vacuumed the carpet and finally stopped,

Turned the key in the lock for one last time, 40 hours on the clock and worth every dime,

I finally completed this holiday home, and the cleaning I achieved all on my own,

I closed the front door and smiled as I went, having cleaned this huge house to the fullest extent…

65   DON'T JUMP IN PUDDLES

"It's my go now, that's so unfair, I was next for a turn,"

Sitting down in a nearby chair, thinking those kids have much to learn,

As I sat a while, just watching them, observing these children at play,

If you could even call it that, more akin to a pecking order display,

Everyone heard their boisterous shouts, from the weakest to the mean,

Their parents just simply lingered about, but no one intervened,

The tallest boy towered over them all, pointing his finger with glee,

"I'm the biggest so hear me roar, and you will all listen to me,"

The smallest child ran off crying, which I thought was kind of funny,

Running so fast, it made me laugh, for he nearly bowled over his mummy,

A petite little lady, about five foot high, she was small, slender and slim,

But as she picked him up and dried his eyes, that was all that mattered to him,

The worries of the day and bullies at play, quickly began to subside,

As they left the park walking hand in hand, he turned to wave goodbye,

"I'll be back again," he yelled out softly, as his little hands frantically waved,

Through tears still falling, he heard a voice calling, "yes come back and I will play,

But only with you, not that big boy too, I'll be waiting for you here tomorrow,"

That turned his frown upside down, how quickly he let go of his sorrow,

He walked away with a smile on his face and a joyful swing in his step,

How eager he was to return to this place, how quickly children forget,

No grudges held, for that they don't know, but somehow all children learn,

How to hold on and never let go, as they feel the depth of its burn,

And its weight on their shoulders, like carrying boulders, a grudge starts a fire inside,

That turns into anger and boils their blood, feeding flames and getting higher,

I turned back to see the kids in the park and wondered at the tallest child,

What was it in him that set off a spark and made him so red faced and wild,

His height perhaps or was it something else, like maybe an inkling of power,

For just a short time, those kids toed the line, for none of them buckled or cowered,

You see size does matter, a great deal in fact, be it stature or a fattened billfold,

It's always the weak and poor that stand back, their soft voices are easily controlled,

From my days of being young, and seeing playgrounds as fun, there was always an order to follow,

And that order remained, completely unchanged, well and truly into all my tomorrows,

Getting up from my seat, I saw a sign on the street, and recalled the boy from today,

The sign simply said, *'try and make an attempt, at never being dismayed,*

It's okay if life, has more wrongs than rights, it's the journey you have on the way,

Start at dawn with a smile, you're only here a short while, so enjoy this most wonderful day,'

The impact we have on the people we meet, is no different to the kids at the park,

Some start off strong and some grow up weak, but we're all born with a beating heart,

And this gives us life, be things wrong or them right, without this we have no chance at all,

As long as it's beating, find value and meaning, be at peace with your stumbles and falls,

Just like we did when we were kids, all our worries were so easily forgot,

By the end of high school, came more adult rules, and some of us just lost the plot,

Our worries mounted more than we could count them, that's when we truly lost sight,

Of what it really means to just simply be, and enjoy each day of our lives,

There's ladders to climb and bills to pay, as we navigate the world of employment,

We rack up more debt with more kids on the way, long gone are the days of enjoyment,

We don't jump in puddles, don't walk in the rain, we just work to merely exist,

It's a constant struggle, every day is the same, but it doesn't have to be like this,

Remember the boy at the park today, who found comfort in the arms of his mummy,

From cradle to grave you will make your way, but the journey is not about money,

We are not our jobs, that's just a means, that's not where our lives are at,

We are living, breathing, human beings, and it's our hearts that make us that…

66   FRIEND OR FOE

Time is a friend to no one, but it gives before it takes,

Slowly sneaks up on you, then one day seals your fate,

As much as this may be true, I can't help but disagree,

I put forward a different view and say time's been a friend to me,

It has patience and perseverance, two qualities I don't possess,

Was quietly on my side, it was time that knew me best,

It taught me many lessons, but took many years to reveal,

I told time what I wanted and it was true to how I feel,

Time ticks the same for everyone, but is said to be going too fast,

Instantaneous yet infinite, time is future, present and past,

You can count on it to be there, you can count on those three hands,

Seconds, minutes and hours, time passes like hourglass sand,

Unbiased, not special to anyone, it just ticks along silently,

Won't judge or misdirect you, it's as true as you want it to be,

You see time is not against us, it gives before it takes,

So treasure the time you're given, and go live it before it's too late…

67   REMEMBER SEPTEMBER

Remember, remember, the first of September, the day you said everything stops,

The next thirty days, are paving the way, to ensure you give up the lot,

It was six months ago you started this journey, on Sunday it's happening for real,

No more minor mishaps, tantrums or spats, you know how much better you'll feel,

You're now on your own, in your new cosy home, so it's the perfect situation,

No outside contact, for anyone to distract, you from dealing with all your frustration,

You did this in March, but you soon fell apart, so now less than in 48 hours,

You'll stay true to your word, implement what you've heard, and no longer be devoured,

You're right on the cusp, of things getting rough, so there's no time left to waste,

Just get a move on, you know what is wrong, like the pimples you see on your face,

To lessen the fears, for the next ten odd years, you know what you need to do,

This journey you're on, is overwhelmingly long, but managed better with the right food,

You've had a good time, many years drinking wine, but you know that cannot go on,

So get off the couch, stop stuffing your mouth, you've been doing this far too long,

You have all you need, to prepare and achieve, this walk down a different path,

Turning fifty years old, means new rules involved, but you have to let go of the past,

You look in the mirror and see someone much thinner, but reality says something else,

You've let yourself go, for reasons unknown and long for your sexy old self,

She didn't go anywhere, she's still hidden in there, under all those baggy clothes,

You have weights and a gym, to make yourself thin, but put it off until tomorrow,

Well tomorrow has come, you will no longer run, away from September the first,

You'll see the month through, you won't come unglued, for things will only get worse,

Your body is changing, so you can't keep remaining, doing nothing till it all goes away,

Learn from your peers, listen to their ideas, make this journey you're on every day,

One you enjoy, not fatigued and annoyed, it really is all up to you,

So remember, remember, the first of September and make sure you see it through…

68   STICKS AND STONES

I was thinking last night for a very long time, about someone who's dear to me,

My eyes wouldn't close, despite how I tried, so I had a very restless sleep,

As the day slowly broke, I eventually woke, to the sound of a notification,

It was a lengthy letter this person had wrote, telling me of her appreciation,

Put her heart and soul into trying to research, a very particular topic,

After reading the many things she had written, I understood and finally got it,

It is something that's been inside of her, since the days of early childhood,

If I had been sitting beside her, I'd give her a hug like a good friend should,

I too poured out my heart and soul, to see if I could change her mind,

But nothing I said could ever console, the hurt she's felt this whole time,

Being called names by hundreds of people, for the past forty odd years,

Drilled a deep hole and left her feeble, unable to dry her own tears,

With little support, she's battled alone, and now decided to change,

A decision she made all on her own, to find a healthier way,

After reading her letter, I too felt better, and wrote a lengthy reply,

I gave my support, with heart felt thoughts, for I just never realised,

This hasty idea is not hasty at all, it's been with her all of her life,

I was too quick, to easily dismiss, years of hurt from words that deride,

It's all good and well to be on the outer and hear people criticise,

But when you're burdened, with years of hurtin', it tears you apart inside,

Today we made a little head way, but there's a very long road to walk,

The truth that we spoke, in the letters we wrote, opened us up to talk,

No hard feelings were had, no matter how bad, the truth can sometimes be,

I hope she has great success with this, and offered support unconditionally,

I realised that some people just wished, there was a gun pointed at their head,

And then that way, they could make the change, for a body they liked instead,

Genetics may have loaded the gun, but their lifestyle pulled the trigger,

Fat makes you fat, it's as simple as that, it's inevitable one will get bigger,

Sticks and stones will break your bones, but words will last forever,

Remember and know you are not alone, we're all in this together…

69 FEAR

How did I manage my chocolate addiction?

Fear.

Fear I would become diabetic and one of my toes gets cut off,

Fear my teeth would fall out, from decay, disease or rot,

Fear is how I managed this addiction and stopped myself eating three blocks,

So fear is how I'll now look at vaping and this time actually stop,

I won't get in the car at 2am and pop down the road for some more,

I'll look at it just like a chocolate bar and the damn thing can stay in the store,

I never ceased sweets altogether, I just said you can't eat this much,

Three blocks in one night is too many, you really have had enough,

Instantly a switch was turned on, just like turning on a light,

From that moment I never faltered, in a way I probably saved my own life,

No magic man had to tell me, I could see my body was telling me,

If you keep eating this much damn sugar, problems for you are guaranteed,

So as for this stick in my hand, I will see it exactly the same,

It's nothing more than a chocolate bar, so I won't continue this game,

We all take our health for granted, until it is taken from us,

Be it vaping, chocolate or junk food, none of us need this damn stuff,

The list goes on for things we don't need, the rubbish that fills up our shops,

I see them all as dangerous goods and that makes it easier to stop,

Imagine seeing in pallets, good grief, what a horrible sight,

To see all the sugar I've consumed, the past forty years of my life,

So I took that thought and imagined, the pallets of vapes I'm yet to smoke,

Every time I think of that simple thought, I remember the words I spoke,

And that's just two temptations, there's been a whole lot more than that,

All these pallets would fill up a street, as well as my pallets of sugar and fat,

So how did they all get to market, because our weakness for them was exposed,

By many an intelligent mind, hundreds of years ago,

But as normal the solution is simple, if we open our eyes to see,

Recognise they're all just illusions, each item a money making scheme,

They made it to market for one thing, but we can all make a choice,

If only we first understood, that silence is also a voice…

70   COUNT TIME NOT GREENBACKS

Saved, cost, spent, lost, words applied to both money and time,

How is it that something so precious, could possibly be so intertwined,

With something so ugly and ruthless, how is this even the case,

Nothing is further from each other, no other words in their place,

We can spend some time as well as lose it, we do this most of the day,

We can lose a dime as well as spend it, as we do each week with our pay,

Time can also come with a cost, when we think back on certain things,

And then there's all the money we've lost, and the sorrow that possibly brings,

You can apply these four basic words, to these two simple nouns,

I realised this from a thought I heard, when I felt myself breaking down,

I woke this morning to a racing heart and my cheeks feeling quite wet,

My dream stunned me out of my slumber and I even started to fret,

I rose in a panic at the thought of a loss, overwhelmed at a choice I had made,

I was frantically trying to recover the cost, from something that I gave away,

I ached at the notion from having no faith, in myself all those years ago,

I sold something good, before it actually could, have the time it needed to grow,

So I asked out aloud what exactly it was, that I wished had never gone,

Did a quick calculation with a few sums, and saw where I had gone wrong,

I would have received a small amount, an estimate of two hundred a year,

That's easily recouped with the money I count, that I spend each week on beer,

So what had I lost that I could not somehow, do again each week if I saved,

It was only damn money, that this mere two hundy, bumped up my yearly wage,

So the last ten years I counted quite quickly, the amount I would've received,

It was all just a bonus that I would have spent, but deep down somehow I still grieved,

Money is printed and can be replaced, but our time here simply cannot,

I dried all my tears and realised all these years, there are many things I've still got,

I've been so bloody lucky and constantly blessed, to have spent these past ten years,

With food on my table and warm clothes to dress, no health scares, problems or fears,

Would I exchange the loss of that two hundy, for a hole dug for me in the dirt,

Time has always been better than money, I woke up and realised its true worth,

Saved or cost, spent or lost, can be applied to our money and time,

One can be earned but the other cannot, so I'm making the most of mine…

71   SHOP CLOSED

There's much to do in the working week,

Make a sausage or two and cut up a sheep,

But if the shop is closed just after lunch,

Everyone knows I've gone out to hunt,

My bag is packed with things I need,

A knife, some bullets and a bag of weed,

It's just me in the bush surrounded by trees,

And my musty scent carried on the breeze,

Deep in the woods I hear a snort,

The cry of an angry warning call:

I'm stronger than you with my mighty tusks,

Step into view if you really must,

I'll pound the earth and prepare for war,

My unbridled worth is what you're hunting for,

You're no match for me, you're just a man,

But that rolled up weed in the palm of your hand,

Is something rather unique to me,

A man with weed is a friend indeed,

Put down your gun, I'll put down my hooves,

Let's smoke some fun and change our mood,

I'll show you the ropes and guide your way,

This is my turf at the end of the day,

Over the years I've met men like you,

Filled with fear when I come into view,

But sometimes what I would really like,

Is to just sit back and smoke all night,

All this fussing and fighting over me,

Is easily fixed with a bag of weed,

I can smell it growing all through the bush,

But I fail in knowing how to burn the kush,

I'm just a boar but you're a man,

Can you shed some light, help me understand,

This scented plant all through my space,

Takes every mammal to their happy place,

When the boys in blue discover your crop,

They burn it down and we inhale the lot,

All the animals here enjoy this stuff,

I tell you mate we can't get enough,

But it's hard to know when you enter the bush,

Are you here to grow more strains of kush,

Or are you here to take me out,

I can sense your fear with my pointy snout,

So I'd like to propose a new idea,

Anytime I smell you come in here,

Stashed in your pack is a bag of green,

Baked cookie snacks just for me,

I'd like to live, as do you,

So let's smoke up a new point of view,

That maybe hunting and killing boars,

Is not what man was put here for,

I'm king of the bush, king of the jungle,

But can't compete against a bullet struggle,

So keep your guns and knives at home,

Let's plant a crop where no one knows,

I'll let you in anytime you like,

You just sit back and smoke your pipe,

And I promise you a safe return,

Look after your crop like you deserve,

I just want weed, you don't have to hunt,

I'm a boar in need, not some silly . . . .

72   GREEDY GREED

In every aspect of all mankind, lays an element of greed in our minds,

Whatever we do or which way we turn, greed inhabits a burning yearn,

Be it desire, wants or needs, its flames of fire will not recede,

From individuals to corporations, it has engulfed every nation,

It's always been our Achilles heel, a drunken driver behind the wheel,

Knows not what thoughtless actions are, oblivious state that can't see far,

For greed is like a one track mind, intoxicating all mankind,

As we turn and twist through roads in life, we never miss the chance to strike,

To shoot off arrows and take our aim, by any means to make a gain,

At wanting more all for ourselves, greed is first as we strive and delve,

To stand on shoulders or stab in backs, greed thrives on endless selfish acts,

It knows not love or understanding, its boundless strength to these withstanding,

And so it's stood the test of time, instilled deep in every mind,

Our instinct to have, hunt and search, we quickly learned its value and worth,

For Greedy Greed is quick to show, it'll get you where you want to go,

Can you imagine how life would be, if all mankind opted to see,

That greed is a vice we do not need, it's a choice we make so we succeed,

But at what price, look at the loss, of human life our biggest cost,

Money, power and even food, our lives devoured by the ones most shrewd,

I sound concerned, but alas I'm not, for I myself have not forgot,

If greed is how we're wired to be, then what will become of humanity,

The complex nature of the human mind, has been like this for all of time,

So make your choices, do what you will, it may be silent, but it wants its fill,

Though greed is not an actual trait, it is an emotion that can dictate,

The paths we're on and roads we take, the love we find and friends we make,

For each and every single person, has the chance to refrain or worsen,

The life of someone they'll never know, plant seeds of love, prosperity for growth,

You'll see one day and then you'll find, that greed need not engulf mankind…

73   PAYOFFS FOR THE PLAY OFF

A spectacular display of bias and deceit,

Yet we continuously support them, week after week,

Who is more to blame, is it us or is it them,

Whilst our wallets reinforce the corruption they defend,

He's even called an umpire, but whose castle does he live,

Residing in the pockets of the ones with most to give,

Does he feather his own cap and pretend he doesn't see,

The mistakes from certain players whom his payoff doesn't feed,

But I was watching intently, through amateur eyes I saw,

What's going on behind the scenes for a team condemned to score,

I even heard the commentator remark on the foul he made,

A forward pass that kicked their arse, was overlooked in this traitorous game,

But the crowd filled up the stadium, every seat worth many bucks,

The other team hindered to win, and if they did, was sheer damn luck,

For the man that rules the field, his final say is all that's heard,

Was permission given to him, with prior approval and affirming words,

Is what played out just an atrocious display, of deceit no one can see,

Is the truth behind the ticket we buy, enabling the powers that be…

ALL FOR MYSELF

Every item you touch and see can only ever be borrowed,

Ownership is a just myth we believe

it's not there when we don't wake tomorrow,

We hoard, we take and we steal, and say we own these things,

When you think about what is real

it's just life and the beauty it brings,

So consider this a reminder, that intangible is what matters most,

Like love and the gift of caring

not what you wear or the wallet you boast,

Does it really give you a better, and more fulfilling life,

How will you be remembered, when your opulence brings others' strife,

Why not share a little more

of the items we have so many,

Give these to the needy and poor

even then we would still have plenty,

But we store like starving squirrels

when there's more than enough to go 'round,

Miss the essence of life as intended

till we're lowered into the ground…

75   CELEBRATING EIGHTY

Today is a celebration and we're here to celebrate you,

The life you've lived, the family you made and the wonderful things you do,

From milking cows to driving trucks, to veggie gardens and loving us,

We could not have wished for a better man, to always be there and understand,

That being a father is the greatest task, and a better Dad we could not have asked,

You started out from humble beginnings, with no TV, hence all your siblings,

In a family that always shared the load, but mischievousness was soon to follow,

You ventured down to see the Mainland, shaved your stubble, what a handsome man,

Down to Kaikoura to be precise, where the local girls looked pretty nice,

So the sea was where you made your home, and bought a house to call your own,

Finding kinas and catching crays, and you fell in love along the way,

With a gorgeous girl you liked and sought, she's the best damn catch you ever caught,

But the old Vauxhall was not ideal, to win the heart of a woman and steal,

Her away on romantic nights, in a car that must be parked just right,

With no reverse gear so you had to push, whilst your beautiful lady sat on her toosh,

Unconventional yes, but at least it worked, she married you for all your worth,

But times back then were bloody hard, so you thought you'd try your hand at darts,

Get free beers from hitting the board, as long as you had the highest score,

So you threw those darts and beat them all, and every Friday they'd come back for more,

But you didn't stop there, you liked it rough, and had the perfect hands for a rugby ruck,

A force on the field as well as the court, no one got in your way playing basketball,

You enriched our lives from the very start, with your great exterior and big soft heart,

When it came to duties of your better half, it's all whips and chains as you dare to laugh,

She taught you well to say "yes dear," and you learned to dodge a clip 'round the ear,

Your daughters' boyfriends thought you were scary, but we knew you were just being wary,

Because fourteen children is a lot of kids, no wonder our boyfriends all ran and hid,

It was only for Mary you toed the line, to be her husband for all of time,

You cut the grass and trimmed the trees, thinking all the while of sport on TV,

And that corner chair that called your name, to finally sit and watch the game,

You're loved for your chuckle and caring smile, your teasing banter and witty style,

You've touched the hearts of all our lives, your grandkids now the apple of your eye,

Your life is filled with so many stories, but the greatest one that takes the glory,

Is the beautiful family that's here today, is because of you and the love you gave,

We really have been very blessed, no one can deny our Dad is the best,

So I'd like to propose that we all toast, to this handsome man we love the most,

A Dad, a husband and a wonderful guy, it's your turn to be the apple of our eye,

You have our hearts in the palm of your hand, so raise your glasses to this special man,

And celebrate his birthday the best way we know, together with love from your whole whanau…

76   GROWING OLD

Growing old has taken me by surprise,

The changes I feel you can see in my eyes,

For they are the window into my soul,

As I've slowly watched my body grow old,

Into this woman that I have become,

From a daughter, to lover and then to a mum,

The dreams I have dreamed and hearts I have melt,

From things I have seen and pain I have felt,

Be it love or loss throughout all my life,

I live my days now for that last sunrise,

If I'm lucky enough to wake up at dawn,

And witness again a new day being born,

I sit back and ponder the life that I've had,

Through all thick and thin, the good and the bad,

For life is not perfect and neither am I,

See into my journey, just look in my eyes,

Millions of memories from near, far and wide,

Now I'm old and grey and wrinkled on the outside,

I remember being fifty and thought I was old,

But the next twenty years, or so I was told,

Will go by so fast you won't even know,

Where time has gone, till you're just skin and bone,

The war wounds of life from years gone past,

Make up all the memories that reside in my heart,

The children I raised with the man that I married,
Now rests in his grave, but his love I still carry,
Our children are grown, some now fathers themselves,
But I feel of no use, like dust on a shelf,
This long road I've walked, I'm now at the end,
Been walking this road since the day I began,
My turn has now come, there's no one in front,
I am of the age where one day I'll lunge,
Forever away into some other place,
Life's a short stay for the whole human race,
We know this at birth that one day it ends,
Each day is a chance to go make amends,
With yourself or with others and heal broken hearts,
You might just discover some long unwalked path,
For people grow old, it's just part of life,
Hear my stories unfold long into the night,
Like the memories I made crossing oceans of wide,
Now one foot's in the grave, I can feel it inside,
Leaves me with one unanswered question to ask,
How does an old lady, sit here waiting to pass,
Fill up her days when she can no longer do,
All the things she did in her youth,
My withered old health is clearly no use,
I know this myself, there's not much I can do,
For growing this old took me by surprise,
And now I await that last sunrise…

77   MY LAST DAY

Is this my last day today, as I get in the car with you and drive,

Will I make it back home nice and safe, I pray this day I will survive,

Accidents happen at any moment, in the quickest blink of an eye,

Distracted drivers on their phones rarely make it out alive,

Not to mention they drive with just one hand, as they go at a hundred k's,

With no room for error, they over correct and meet an early grave,

We see this on the news at night, we hear this all the time,

People crash and lose their life, only their memory left behind,

Alcohol, speed or just stupidity, they underestimate what they're driving,

Phones away and two hands always, if you'd like to keep surviving,

I've heard my friends sometimes say, "by myself I'll be on my phone",

If it was just you, that's maybe okay, but you're not on the roads alone,

There's people coming the other way, so what about what they're doing,

When drivers take their eyes off the roads, it's danger you're pursuing,

These vehicles weigh over a tonne and need only just a second,

To slip out of control, and possibly roll, so make sure your eyes are checkin',

Any survivor that lives to tell the tale, has spoken of this split,

Second it took, when they didn't look, and next thing they were hit,

To get a licence is too damn easy and no follow up lessons are had,

For decades long, we just drive along, no matter how good or bad,

Impatience grows, on all our roads, and always someone dies,

Won't wait to pass, so they sit up your arse, and then you see them fly,

There's no respect for the power of cars, people just push a peddle,

They think they're safe inside this thing that's only made of metal,

Until one day when they're upside down, and then they realise,

Holy shit that happened so fast, we're lucky we didn't die,

I'm an anxious passenger, but a respectful driver and keep my eyes ahead,

On the road, wherever I go, for I don't plan on being dead,

I cater for the reckless drivers, that are on the other side,

Driving one handed, fluffing around, and not looking with their eyes,

There's only so much I can do, but I want nothing to distract,

Not on my phone, even if I'm alone, I want that second so I can react…

DAYLIGHT SAVINGS BLUES

The sun comes out and we get up, then start our day with our work stuff,

Feed yourself and then your pets, head off to work and do your best,

We keep to schedules and mind the clock,

But daylight savings can sometimes rock,

The boat we're in and I wonder why,

Twice a year they change the time,

Can't it remain and just simply stay,

Always for the daylight save,

Why switch back and make it dark, all so suddenly may I ask,

We're happiest when the sun is out, after work parties and drinks to shout,

Crank up the barbie and crack a beer,

But then all of a sudden it disappears,

Thrust into darkness before we know,

Daylight savings doesn't have to go,

Why can't the clock just stay right there, why change it back when we're not prepared,

I think we'd all be better off,

To remain on time with the savings clock,

Then naturally winter would slowly come,

And keep the rhythm for everyone…

79   TURNING TWENTY ONE

You came into this world as small as can be,

We nursed you and kissed you so tenderly,

Through the tantrums, tears and the terrible three's,

You grew into this young man today that we see,

Remembering moments like your friend's broken leg,

From a play wrestle fight, he toppled off the bunk bed,

You carefully nursed him back to being good,

Helped him along in any way that you could,

A supportive wee boy and a brave little man,

Always thinking of others and lending a hand,

So courageous and caring, you're a wonderful son,

We are so proud of you and who you've become,

Working hard at your studies to attain your degree,

Achieved all your goals so diligently,

Chaperoned your sweetheart to the high school ball,

Every head turned as you entered the hall,

The stunning young girl you had at your side,

You may choose one day to be your bride,

A fabulous husband and father you'll make,

And maybe some grandkids one day would be great,

We've watched you grow from a boy to a man,

From pushing toy trucks to driving a work van,

Fills us with pride as we honour our son,

And celebrate this day as you turn twenty one…

80   SWEET DREAMS

As long as we're living we are always learning, it's just something that we do,

The things I've learned I learned from friends, like the one I found in you,

I could open up and share my heart and all my deepest thoughts,

You guided me through troubled times with the life lessons you taught,

The memories we made, from the friendship you gave, to me I'll always hold dear,

We may be apart, but you're still in my heart, and cherished for all of my years,

The one true gent I have ever met, and a handsome man at that,

You helped me see the forest through the trees and you never turned your back,

I remember the day that we first met and the wonderful stories you told,

I chatted away and together we'd vent, it was then my heart you stole,

I knew from then on we would always be friends, no matter our struggles or strife,

For someone like you, with a heart so true, would always be in my life,

I'll carry your memory wherever I go, you will never be forgotten,

I miss you more than you'll ever know, sweet dreams my beautiful Scotland…

81   PLAYING THE FIELD

It's no longer relevant if it's false or it's true,
A thought was planted and that's hard to undo,
I am not a doll nor am I a toy,
I won't be controlled and for this you're annoyed,
But I do understand the lines and the lies,
As you bed at will what's in front of your eyes,
The field you are in is a treacherous place,
A smile hides the scorn on everyone's face,
Feelings redundant as you quickly move on,
Leaving you empty as the day is long,
The needs and the wants of the loneliest man,
Will betray his own heart and then force his hand,
To go to great lengths to commit an act,
Realise it's too late and there's no turning back,
You fooled yourself and nearly fooled me,
Into believing everything I believed,
Time soon revealed the ugly truth of your fate,
Now I simply refuse to share the same space,
So ask me the question, where did you go wrong,
Why not just admit that you shouldn't have gone,
To the field where you're playing and expect me to stay,
Wait for your love as your heart goes astray,
So whether it's true or whether it's not,
Don't play me the fool and assume I forgot,
Your eyes may be open but your heart is closed off,
No loyalty spoken, so everything stops…

82 FOOL IN LOVE

Was I a fool to think you wanted me, a fool to think that way,

I watched your heart a flutter with the new girl yesterday,

Her long dark hair, you stopped and stared, and offered her your time,

Since we met, you were the perfect gent, and I hoped that you'd be mine,

I pictured you laying next to me, nestled in your arms,

Listening to all your crazy stories and falling for your charms,

But this was not to be, so I'll simply find another,

Leave you with your newest friend and no longer be a bother,

I won't join you for a movie or wish to play your game,

You made your bed, now lie in it, to you it's all the same,

All it takes is a pretty face and you hope she'll give you more,

But she wasn't there in her underwear when you knocked upon her door,

You soon found out you're a bloody fool, a bigger one than me,

That girl was never interested, she was completely out of your league,

And you wonder why you're single, it's because of your wandering heart,

You missed what was in front of you, that I loved you from the start,

The new girl's gone and so have I, you're on your own again,

Is this why I see such an abundance of so many lonely men…

83   JUST ONE NIGHT

My heart skips a beat when I hear from you, and to my phone my eyes are glued,

I read your message several times, dreaming and hoping that you'll be mine,

But I gave up on love years ago, never trusting anyone as far as I could throw,

So I only go out to have some fun, just live in the moment when I meet someone,

Rest in their arms for just one night, make sure I'm gone by dawn's first light,

A memory is made from that moment on, to be nothing more than a moment gone,

My heart is full yet it's still so empty, this tender heart has endured plenty,

But who can mend my broken wings, someone who's been through similar things,

Till then I'll keep it tucked away, and maybe again I'll share it someday,

So keep on sending your little texts, my heart skips a beat in hope of what's next…

84   BUCKET OF GOLD

What do you find value in, is it a rainbow or to hear a bird sing,

If I had nothing and you had it all, does that make you great and me rather small,

If I had a bucket of gold to mind, as I went away for a very long time,

Would it still be there when I got back, and not traded in for something you lack,

What if it was a bucket of rocks, would it still need securing with key and lock,

What if it was just a bucket of leaves, little value to you but important to me,

Would I be reassured and guaranteed, you'd look after my bucket for as long as I need,

You would not trade it in or it ever be sold, be it leaves or rocks or a bucket of gold,

So what do you find value in, reflect on this now and start to begin,

Sifting through all of your buckets in life, what precious items you'd die for and fight,

If you only had just a few items to take, set off on a journey to a new life you make,

You would soon discover the value you find, in each little item that you left behind,

We all have our different buckets in life, to someone they're wrong, but to others they're right,

What I value most may be different for you, it all just depends on one's point of view…

85   ADVERTISING

Why do people go under the knife, is it to look better and feel alright,

How do we know what's in store, when we chop ourselves up, who is it for,

Where was this notion derived, is it from you or the girl at your side,

As I asked myself this question, my life long partner made the suggestion,

If they liked you from the start, there is no need for tearing apart,

Your face, your chest, your thighs, just love yourself and you'll realise,

This notion has come from a place, of advertising the most perfect face,

These images simply aren't real, they're out to make money and they will steal,

Whatever they can from your life, don't fall for the trap and go under the knife,

You're perfect in all that I see, your aging flaws mean nothing to me,

For when you look deep inside, you see inner beauty and know that I'm right,

So if they liked you from the start, then aging together should be the best part...

TRULY IS BLIND

I know what it is,
I know what it does,
It burns like fire our desire for love,
It'll hit you like a tidal wave and leave you on the sand,
You feel it calling out to you 'come and take my hand',
Sometimes love is just like that,
Somehow it has its own mind,
Plan as you will,
But things must still,
Play out as love's designed,
It can soothe a cold breeze with the warmth of its glow,
Snatch you up and you won't even know,
Like the gentle flakes from a cold winter's snow,
You won't feel the touch of cupid's arrow,
Can you see what it does,
Do you see what I mean,
It just turns up like the middle of a dream,
Not there yesterday, wasn't there before,
Then feelings come flooding and return you to shore,
When someone is calling 'come take my hand',
You feel love gently falling like waves on the sand,
For it conquers all and binds us together,
As we answer the call, our desire for pleasure,
It's been like this since the beginning of time,
The beauty of love, it truly is blind…

DESIRE FOR YOU

My desire for you gets stronger each day,

A moment without you is to my dismay,

You're truly too much, but I can't let you go,

Think of you always, but you'd never know,

From the minute I wake to my last thought at night,

I simply must have you every day of my life,

I've attempted to go just one day or two,

And be by myself, instead of with you,

But the feeling's too strong and you're with me again,

My desire for you, just never ends,

I must leave you be, but I just can't let go,

I want myself back, much more than you know,

What you've created is beyond my control,

My need for you grows and rips through my soul,

So tomorrow I vow to start anew,

And end my love of tasty rich food…

88   INCORRIGIBLE ENEMY

I remember my last days vividly as if seeing my first sunrise,

It was like a cloud of confusion had been lifted before my eyes,

I woke to the hidden benefits, which I longed to always feel,

Each day there's new found energy, for years I let you steal,

No longer will you drain me nor rob me of tomorrow,

My wealth and health will be the first to relinquish years of sorrow,

I can see the free edge starting to form upon my fingertips,

And cease all that you've taken through your poison on my lips,

A simple thought was all it took to make this needed switch,

The benefits and positives will just empower and enrich,

My precious life here on in, and every day forever more,

I feel a burst of energy now, like I've never felt before,

The ripple effect of the problems you bring, echoed in my mind,

I could feel the change within me as you drained me one last time,

Disguised as something special, a desire that we need,

You're simply just a poison, a legal social disease,

I was so immersed in your world for over thirty years,

You may have been an income, but you evoked many tears,

I gravitated to your wicked ways as you gently crept in slowly,

What I learned from being with you, is that you feed on prey that's lonely,

A few kind words from a pretty face, they were putty in your hands,

You raised their egos out to space, and they succumbed to your commands,

To me you were only just a job, tried to keep my distance far,

But sobriety never lasted long, working behind a bar,

I was not immune, to the crowded room, I too wanted what they had,

And jiggle away to the latest tunes, aching to feel glad,

Sensing your poison giving life to the blood cells in my veins,

Oblivious to ever notice, my demeanour slowly change,

Friend or foe, only I can know, which one I want you to be,

You were my master and I your slave, an incorrigible enemy…

89   WONDERFUL IMAGINATION

Nothing is ever for sure, that's the only sure thing that I know,

The choices we make today may not be fit for tomorrow,

For life is always evolving, around the corner we cannot see,

The problems we think we are solving, could sometimes be damaging,

We learn through mistakes and growing, that simply happens with time,

Every experience we have is worth knowing, through these is how we're defined,

If we all had a crystal ball, would that prove things any better,

Avoid our stumbles and falls, to ensure a perfect life forever,

How would we indulge certain appetites, like dreaming and imagination,

If all that occurred was foretold, predicted for every situation,

The greatest mysteries of life, lay in the depths of our minds,

To discover and see for ourselves, is simply how life was designed,

We must never know tomorrow, it can only be wished and dreamed,

If we did it would bring us sorrow, and undo what life really means,

That's why today is a present, and the next day is only a gift,

The future is undetermined, not purposed for us to predict,

What we have are these two things, and no instructions of any kind,

Just the wonders of our imagination and the dreams in our beautiful minds…

90   BEST GIFT OF ALL

The nineteenth of December, just five days out till Christmas,

Maybe one day I will look back, and actually say I miss this,

Coming together once a year, is all about this special day,

And as more time disappears, I've learned some things along the way,

Many people find value in Christmas, in ways I never thought,

The joy of fulfilling a wish list, hunting for gifts they cannot afford,

But for me the focus was only, simply on just turning up,

Making the effort to be there, wasn't worried about the other stuff,

I seldom buy Christmas presents, because the best gift of all is me,

Just the human being presence, of being with our families,

Gifts come wrapped in a box, and we end up in one too,

As you untie the ribbon's knot, remember life is a gift for you,

So don't waste your time or money, on purchases from a shop,

You're already the best damn present, your friends and family ever got…

WORK OF ART

I could write about love till the sun comes up

and write some more till it's down,

Tell everyone of this wondrous feeling

that can turn your whole world around,

It can mend the heart of a wounded soul

and open up their eyes,

Or take you away to a dreamy place

and be your morning sunrise,

No power on earth or iron will

can ever break its bond,

No matter the strength of a thousand men

love is just too strong,

It is quite simply a wondrous thing

this feeling in one's heart,

Love can conquer anything,

it's a beautiful work of art…

EVERY BREATH

Life is apparent in each breath we take,

It's easily forgotten and a deadly mistake,

Inhale the air and feel your chest rise,

The beauty of life

is before your very eyes,

So pause for a moment and remember this,

With each breath you take

your life can exist,

Hold it too long and things turn to blue,

But take a deep breath

you'll feel so renewed,

Each day and each moment of every hour,

The air that we breathe

is giving us power,

So much so in fact it enables our lives,

Without each breath we could not survive,

So take not for granted

the air that we breathe,

Remember this most precious thing

that we need…

93   TWENTY FOUR MILLION

An employer addresses his staff, as he casually sits down to ask,

If you won 24 million, would you still come in tomorrow,

Come to work, in your ironed shirt, watch your colleagues beg and borrow,

I bet you 24 million, you would not do such a thing,

The moment you saw the perfect score, immense joy these numbers would bring,

So the point I make is simple, it's not difficult to see,

The money you scored has opened up doors, and may possibly set you free,

So don't forget today's frustrations, that exist within these walls,

Whilst your colleagues still remain here, in jobs they don't want at all,

So next time your work mate falters, and stuffs up a simple task,

They're here for the pay, at the end of the day, so don't kick them up the arse,

If I won 24 million, there's no way you'd see me again,

But I'm sure I'd find many people, who would want to be my friend,

Believe me I'd be choosy, so I would leave a legacy,

That money's too much for one person, I'd share mine for eternity…

94   MY LOVE OF RHYME

Sometimes I rhyme as I'm thinking the words, then write them all down these words I just heard,

It's easy for me as I don't have to speak, it naturally comes these words that I think,

I love spending my time on poems to write, passing each day rhyming into the night,

Some are amazed at the speed I achieve, so many poems to me it's a breeze,

We all have a talent we like to display, poems are mine so I write them each day,

Filled several books in over a year, published my first one that you're reading here,

There's still more to do to have the book of my dreams, from start to finish of unique poetry,

Every paragraph, page and each single line, an entire book that completely rhymes,

If I focus right now I just may achieve, the thing that I want and truly succeed,

So working two jobs was quite a damn lot, I'm broke as hell, but I needed to stop,

Personalised poetry is what I want to do, write on the spot, here and now impromptu,

Just name the topic and leave me to it, I'll come up with something because you can't do it,

This is my passion, my goal is to write, staying up late bringing stories to life,

So if you would like to see that I could, write a poem for you that is really good,

Send me an email and tell me what, you'd like me to write, I'll give it all that I've got…

95   UNIQUE POETRY

How do I do this, is it for you or for me,

Should I just give my talent to the world for free,

Many thoughts are running through my mind,

And another day simply passes me by,

I still have my job to maintain my life,

But spend my evenings writing each night,

Will I find somebody who likes my work,

Will anyone recognise their worth,

Is there an audience for my rhyming words,

If I wrote about sex, would that be heard,

From dawn to dusk it is everywhere,

Strip ourselves down till naked and bare,

Many people are making a dollar or two,

The beautiful ones get millions of views,

I can write about beauty all day long,

Maybe my poems could make a hit song,

But as for my beauty, well I do not possess,

The standard required of what sells best,

The world can be such a hard, cruel place,

For those who don't have a beautiful face,

All that I have is here in my hand,

Just a pen to capture and understand,

What you are feeling and write it all down,

Bring your thoughts to life with verbs and nouns,

It would be designed and written for you,

For writing uniquely is what I can do,

Or you could enquire and purchase from me,

A poem or two from what you have seen,

Check out my website and have a good look,

At dozens of poems that only took,

A few minutes or so for me to write,

See if you find something there that you like,

If not, you could email and simply just ask,

I'd write something for you, real super fast,

Anniversaries, birthdays or just for your lover,

There's no topic at all that I cannot cover,

For a reasonable fee, I'd write it right now,

Any subject, verse or even your vows,

I know you'd be happy with what you'll receive,

And pleased you discovered my unique poetry…

"A THOUGHT CAN GIVE YOU ENERGY
A THOUGHT CAN BE DEPLETING
A MILLION THOUGHTS RUN THROUGH OUR MINDS
WHICH ONE OF THEM HAS MEANING
CAN WE DETERMINE RIGHT FROM WRONG
THESE THOUGHTS THAT HOLD SUCH POWER
SEND YOU INSANE
THINKING OVER AGAIN
RELENTLESS HOUR BY HOUR
BUT WE ARE NOT OUR THOUGHTS
AN ENTITY TO OVERCOME
LOOK AT THEM OBJECTIVELY
OR YOUR THOUGHTS WILL OVERRUN"

Copyright T.A.McAlister 19Jan2022

THANK YOU

Laying here and quietly listening to the raindrops falling down,

I imagine seeing each one glistening, as they gently touch the ground,

Every single tiny raindrop is like a letter in my mind,

I see each one then slowly forming, words to make a rhyme,

And then I watch them come together and picture all these words,

Like puddles forming all around me, a rhyme is then observed,

Our minds do not know boundaries, or any limitations,

It's free to be whatever it sees, an endless imagination,

Rhymes allow my mind to wander and you read what it creates,

Some are fantasy, some are true, they're just words that illustrate,

Embellished stories to entertain, but always they're designed,

To show the reader these detailed thoughts, inside a mind that rhymes,

So I'd like to express my appreciation, for the time you've taken to read,

After many years of deliberation, for this journey to finally succeed,

And put on show the stories I've written, a compilation over time,

Thank you kindly for all you've given and your interest in my rhyming mind…

"The True Kiwi Way" - Uncle D   (Waltz time)

V1 D   G   D
   If you are a kiwi, right down to the bone
       D   A
   No matter where you live, New Zealand's still home
       D   G
   So whether you're here, or you're so far away
              D   A   D   D
   You will always do things, "The True Kiwi Way"

Chorus:
           D   *G*   *D*
So stand proud as a Kiwi, to call New Zealand your home
            D   *A*
Stand proud and remember, you'll not be standing alone
       D   *G*
One people one nation, at the end of the day
          D   *A*   *D*   *D*
All proud that we do things, "The True Kiwi Way"

V2 D   G   D
   It's everyday people, just like you and me
          D   A
   Who make up New Zealand, for the whole world to see
          D   G
   So be proud and remember, at the end of the day
             D   A   D   D
   That we are all Kiwis, living "The True Kiwi Way"

CHORUS

V3 D   G   D
   No matter your colour, or your place of birth
        D   A
   We are all Kiwis, from the greatest place on earth
             D   G
   And we'll all stand united, at work rest or play
              D   A   D   D
   And we'll always do things "The True Kiwi Way"

CHORUS (x2)

T.K.W written by my Dad, Darryll McAlister, 2003
pen name Uncle D

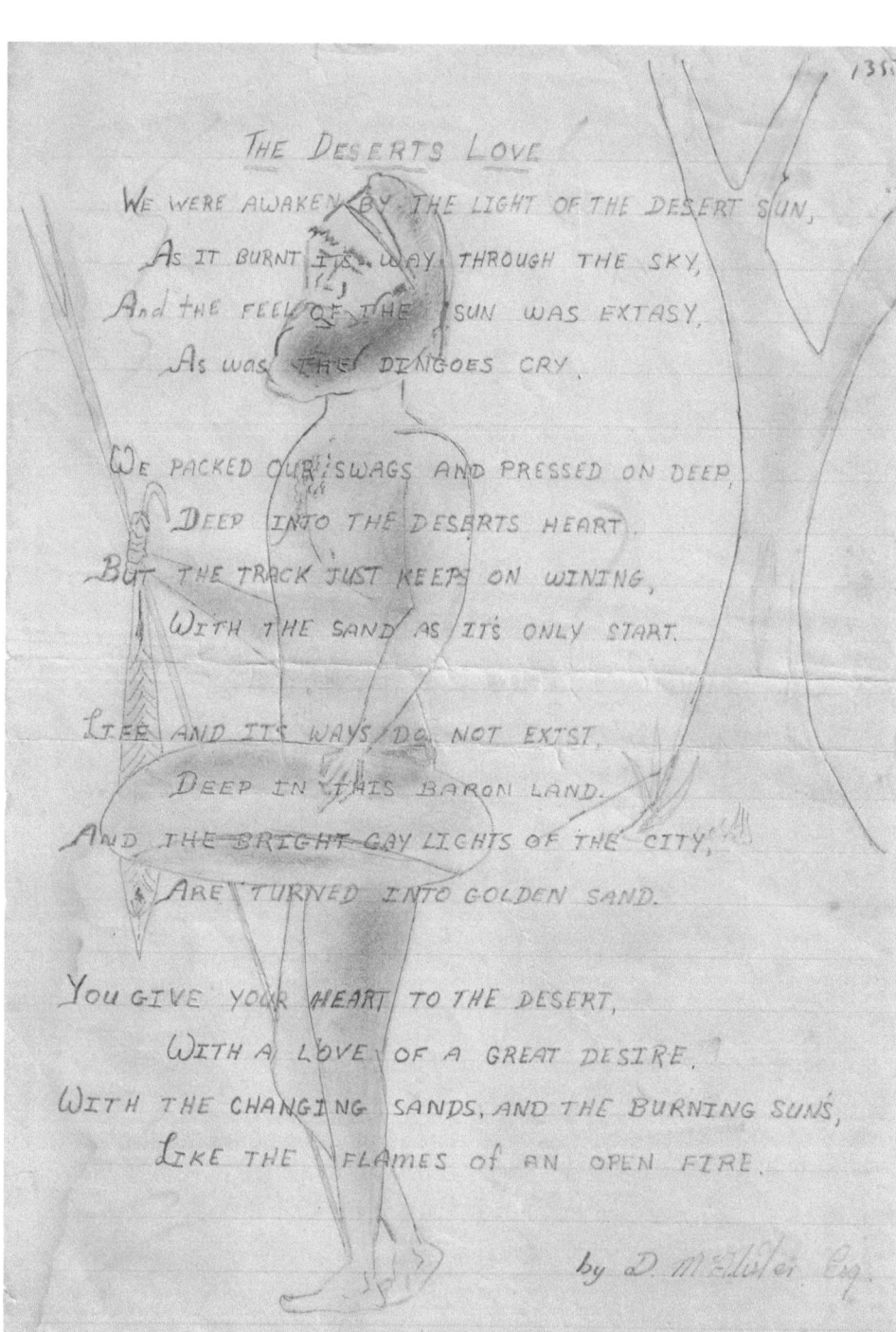

The Deserts Love

We were awaken by the light of the desert sun,
 As it burnt its way through the sky,
And the feel of the sun was extasy,
 As was the dingoes cry.

We packed our swags and pressed on deep,
 Deep into the deserts heart.
But the track just keeps on wining,
 With the sand as its only start.

Life and its ways do not exist,
 Deep in this baron land.
And the bright gay lights of the city,
 Are turned into golden sand.

You give your heart to the desert,
 With a love of a great desire.
With the changing sands, and the burning suns,
 Like the flames of an open fire.

by D. McAlister Esq.

THE BEAST.

HE STANDS SO ERECT WITH MUSCLES OF STEAL
AND HIS EYES COVER EVERY INCH
WITH THE FORCOMING OF HIS HUNTER
THE great beasts MUSCLES FLINCH

HIS GREAT COAT BLOWS IN THE MORNING BREEZE
AND IS WORTH A FORTUNE IN ANY STATE
THIS GREAT ANIMAL IS BECOMING SLOWLY PRESERVED
BUT TIME IS COMING LATE.

WITH THE CRACK OF THE BULLET FROM THE HUNTERS GUN
THE GREAT BEAST BOUNDS OUT OF SIGHT.
ONLY TO BOUND FOR A DAY OR SO
FOR DEATH IS THE GREAT ROOS PLIGHT

www.ingramcontent.com/pod-product-compliance
Lightning Source LLC
Chambersburg PA
CBHW041613220426
43670CB00001B/3